:ven Holzner

Sams **Teach Yourself**

HTML5

in **10 Minutes**

SAMS | 800 East 96th Street, Indianapolis, Indiana 46240

Sams Teach Yourself HTML5 in 10 Minutes

International Standard Book Number-10: 0-672-33333-3

International Standard Book Number-13: 978-0-672-33333-0

Library of Congress Cataloging-in-Publication Data

Holzner, Steven.

    Sams teach yourself HTML5 in 10 minutes / Steven Holzner.

      p. cm.

    ISBN 978-0-672-33333-0 (pbk.)

    1. HTML (Document markup language) I. Title. II. Title: Teach yourself HTML5 in 10 minutes.

    QA76.76.H94H647 2011

    006.7'4—dc22

                           2010045971

Printed in the United States of America

First Printing: December 2010

13   12   11   10   4   3   2   1

Trademarks

Warning and Disclaimer

Bulk Sales

Sams Publishing offers excellent discounts on this book when ordered in quantity for bulk purchases or special sales. For more information, please contact

    U.S. Corporate and Government Sales
    1-800-382-3419
    corpsales@pearsontechgroup.com

For sales outside of the U.S., please contact

    International Sales
    international@pearsoned.com

Editor In Chief
Mark Taub

Aquisitions Editor
Mark Taber

Development Editor
Songlin Qiu

Managing Editor
Sandra Schroeder

Project Editor
Mandie Frank

Copy Editor
Barbara Hacha

Indexer
Heather McNeill

Proofreader
Debbie Williams

Publishing Coordinator
Vanessa Evans

Composition
Mark Shirar

Book Designer
Gary Adair

Table of Contents

About the Author

Steven Holzner is the award-winning author of 108 computer books and a contributing editor at *PC Magazine*. His books have sold 2.5 million copies and have been translated into 22 languages. He specializes in Web topics such as Facebook, banner ads, Google, Yahoo, and MSN pay-per-click campaigns, viral marketing, usenet marketing, and more. He also owns four apartment buildings that he markets exclusively on the Web (direct emails, banner ads, pay-per-click, email autoresponders, Craig's list, rent.com, and about ten other advertising sites) to find tenants.

We Want to Hear from You!

As the reader of this book, you are our most important critic and commentator. We value your opinion and want to know what we're doing right, what we could do better, what areas you'd like to see us publish in, and any other words of wisdom you're willing to pass our way.

You can email or write me directly to let me know what you did or didn't like about this book—as well as what we can do to make our books stronger.

Please note that I cannot help you with technical problems related to the topic of this book, and that due to the high volume of mail I receive, I might not be able to reply to every message.

When you write, please be sure to include this book's title and author as well as your name and phone or email address. I will carefully review your comments and share them with the author and editors who worked on the book.

Email: webdev@samspublishing.com

Mail: Mark Taber
         Associate Publisher
         Sams Publishing
         800 East 96th Street
         Indianapolis, IN 46240 USA

Reader Services

Visit our website and register this book at www.informit.com/register for convenient access to any updates, downloads, or errata that might be available for this book.

Introduction

Welcome to HTML5, the new edition of HTML.

Many people are saying that it's about time for HTML5—HTML 4.01 was completed in 1999. Others are saying that what HTML5 offers is just too good to pass up. We hope you'll agree with both opinions.

HTML5 goes beyond all previous versions of HTML in scope and power. In fact, its biggest additions are in the scripting realm, not in the traditional realm of HTML elements at all. So if you're expecting just a list of new HTML elements, this book may surprise you. HTML has learned about JavaScript, and puts it to work extensively.

For example, HTML5 supports drag and drop, but you've got to use a scripting language like JavaScript to make it work. HTML5 also supports a Canvas control in which you can draw—using JavaScript. There are many more such areas that we'll see come alive in the new HTML.

What's in This Book

This book gives you a guided tour of the new features of HTML. We assume you know the previous version of HTML—HTML 4.01—well enough so that we can discuss only what's new in version 5. Here are the stops on your guided tour:

- ▶ Lesson 1, "Essential HTML5"—In this lesson, you'll get an overview of HTML5, as well as learning the rules for constructing an HTML5 document.

- ▶ Lesson 2, "Drawing with the Canvas Element"—Here you'll learn how to use JavaScript to draw in HTML5's new Canvas element.

- ▶ Lesson 3, "Dragging and Dropping with HTML5"—This lesson shows how to make items in Web pages "draggable" with the mouse.

▶ Lesson 4, "Web Form Controls"—HTML5 includes new controls
(controls are elements such as radio buttons or check boxes that
the user interacts with), including new telephone and datetime
controls. We'll put them to work here.

▶ Lesson 5, "Inline Editing"—With HTML5, you can edit the text
contents of elements such as <div> or <span> interactively, and
we'll see how here.

▶ Lesson 6, "Working With Browser History"—In this lesson, we
take a look at the built-in support in HTML for navigating the
browser through its history, revisiting pages it has already been to.

▶ Lesson 7, "Getting the Point Across with Messaging"—HTML5
lets you send messages from one document to another, and we'll
get a glimpse into how that works here, by sending messages
from one document to another that appears in an <iframe> in the
first document.

▶ Lesson 8, "Using Video and Audio"—Some of the most exciting
aspects of HTML5 are the <video> and <audio> elements. We'll
see how to play videos and audio using them in this lesson.

▶ Lesson 9, "Web Storage"—One thing web page authors have
missed with traditional HTML and JavaScript is some place to
store data between page accesses by the user. HTML5 gives you
a couple of options that we'll take a look at in this lesson.

▶ Lesson 10, "The New HTML5 Elements"—HTML5 comes with
many new elements in addition to the ones we've already covered
in the book, and we'll see them here.

What You Need

HTML5 is still in its infancy, so it takes a little patience. In particular, browser support is still spotty, which means that not all features are supported in all browsers. We'll be working with five browsers in this book: Firefox, Chrome, Safari, Opera, and Internet Explorer.

Each time we cover an HTML5 feature in this book, we list which browser(s) currently supports it, so if you want to put something to work, you might want to check browser support first.

To read this book, you'll need to have a working knowledge of HTML 4.01 (the current standard version) and JavaScript. You don't need to be an expert at either of these, but you will need a working knowledge.

For the most part, all the examples in this book can be run simply by opening an HTML document in your browser from your hard disk. However, two short examples (webforms.html and webforms.php in Lesson 4) require the use of a web server—when we show how to read data on the server from the new web form controls and when we store data in the web session that the browser creates with a web server. To use these two examples, you'll need to upload them to a web server; otherwise, no special preparation is needed to run any of the examples in this book.

That's all you need to get started, so let's jump in and do just that in Lesson 1.

LESSON 1

Essential HTML5

Welcome to HTML5, the new exciting version of HTML5 that pushes the web-development envelope. Packed with features, HTML5 is winning legions of fans as it goes beyond what HTML has been traditionally able to do. In this lesson, we'll get an overview of what HTML5 can do and start the process of creating HTML5 documents.

Welcome to HTML5

HTML5 breaks down the barrier between HTML and scripting. HTML5 turns out to be very script intensive. It has a bunch of new elements and attributes, but the major push in HTML5 has to do with features that you can access only through scripting.

Whether it's dragging and dropping items, drawing in a canvas, storing data in the browser between page accesses, browser history, or any of more than a dozen other topics, HTML5 relies on scripting—and that means JavaScript for most people—more than ever before. To make HTML5 work, you have to use scripting.

That's a good thing, because incorporating the new capabilities, which demand scripting, into HTML itself means that browser manufacturers will have to support those new capabilities. Often, what's possible in JavaScript varies widely from browser to browser, and requiring a lot of scripting support in HTML will make support for the new features uniform across all browsers.

All versions of HTML, including HTML5, are products of the World Wide Web Consortium, or W3C (www.w3.org), which is composed of the people responsible for putting together the various versions of the HTML specifications. The version before HTML5, which is HTML 4.01, came out in 1999.

Each W3C specification, called a recommendation (W3C is careful not to consider itself a standards-creating body, so they call their specifications recommendations), goes through several steps.

First comes Note status, where some people at W3C start discussing some issue. Then a Working Draft of a specification is created, and the W3C invites comments. Next comes a Candidate Recommendation, and then the final version of a W3C specification, the Recommendation.

All these steps are posted online for you to peruse. HTML5 is in Working Draft format at the time this book was written, and you can see the specification as it stands at W3C, http://www.w3.org/TR/html5/ (which is just a long table of contents of links to other documents).

We'll be working from the W3C HTML5 Working Draft in this book. Because it's still relatively early in HTML5's history, browser support is spotty. All the features we'll take a look at in this book are supported in one or more browsers, but not in all browsers (we'll be looking at Internet Explorer, Chrome, Firefox, Opera, and Safari). For each feature, we'll list which browsers support it.

Let's get an overview now of HTML5 capabilities.

Drawing With the Canvas Element

The Canvas element has been long awaited. As its name implies, you can use this element to draw on, and that can mean drawing some complex figures. You can draw lines, circles, arcs, rectangles, curves, and more. You can color figures as you like them and even insert images.

The Canvas control is a powerful one because it brings dynamic graphics to Web pages, displaying graphics that you can change in response to the user's actions. This element relies extensively on JavaScript, as do most HTML5 elements, so you do your drawing in JavaScript.

For most figures, you use a simple function call in JavaScript, such as lineTo(), stroke(), or fill(). So you're drawing from JavaScript, as we'll see in Lesson 2.

Dragging and Dropping

Another eagerly anticipated feature in HTML5 is drag and drop. Formerly, dragging and dropping items in a web page relied on ad hoc JavaScript, which had to be written differently for every browser. Now dragging and dropping will be uniform across all browsers.

If you've ever written drag and drop code in JavaScript, you know what a huge relief this will be. No longer will you have to test which browser your code is executing in and decide what code to run—that for the Internet Explorer, Firefox, and so on.

In HTML5, most visual elements have a draggable attribute, which, if set to true, allows users to drag and drop the element—provided they implement the dragging and dropping in JavaScript. We'll see all about drag and drop in Lesson 3.

Getting Data With the New Web Form Controls

HTML5 comes stocked with a number of new controls, extending considerably the controls already available in HTML (such as check boxes, option buttons, and so on). For example, there is now a color picker, an email field, a datetime control, and even a telephone number control.

These controls offer a lot of much-needed power to HTML. For example, the color control usually displays a color picker where the user can select colors just by clicking them. The datetime control usually displays a small calendar that the user can select dates from. The actual implementation of these controls is up to the individual browser manufacturers, but many of these new controls are already being implemented, and we'll take a look at them in Lesson 4.

Edit Web Pages on the Fly

Web pages become more interactive with HTML5, and that includes letting the user edit text in a web page.

Remembering With Browser History

HTML5 also allows you to get a handle on the browser's history—that is, what pages it's been to.

In Lesson 6, we're going to take a look at what browser history means in HTML5. And it's not just a trail of pages either—you can store data between page accesses, so that data is available to you when you return to a page.

That's very powerful, because until now, browsers have always started off with a clean slate whenever they come to—or come back to—a page. Now you can start storing data that will persist even between page accesses.

Saying Hello With Interdocument Messaging

HTML5 also lets you send messages between various parts of a document, even when those parts actually come from different documents. That is, you might display a web page in an <iframe> in another page. Now you can send text messages to the contained document, which you couldn't do before.

In fact, it's now possible to send messages to pages displayed in elements like <iframe> or <div> elements even if those pages come from a completely different domain, which was quite illegal until now.

Awesome Audio and Video

A big part of HTML5 is the video and audio support. The new <video> element displays videos, and the <audio> element plays soundtracks—all without the use of browser plug-ins like those for Flash or QuickTime.

These new elements are the subject of Lesson 8. In that lesson, we'll see which browser supports what audio and video formats at this point. For example, as of this writing, Firefox, Opera, and Chrome all support the Theora video format for the <video> element, which plays videos with the extension .ogg, as well as the VP8 video codec.

In Lesson 8, we'll not only get videos to play with the <video> element, but we'll also see how to convert common video formats into formats that will play using that element.

Making Use of Web Storage

One of the things that HTML/JavaScript authors have missed in the past is somewhere to store data between page accesses. That is, when you reopen a page that includes standard JavaScript, all the variables in your JavaScript are reset to their original values.

That's fixed in HTML5, where you have the option of saving data in the browser, as well as in the browser's session with the server. The details are coming up in Lesson 9.

In Lesson 9 we'll create an example where all you have to do to store text locally in the browser is to enter that text in a text field and click the Store button. Then you can navigate away from the page and come back to it later. When you come back later, you can click the Get button, and the data in the text field will be restored.

HTML/JavaScript authors now have the ability to store data between page accesses. Very cool.

Using the New Elements

What would a new version of HTML be without new HTML elements? Here are the HTML elements that are new in HTML5—and we'll take a look at them in Lesson 10:

- ▶ <article>
- ▶ <aside>
- ▶ <audio>
- ▶ <canvas>
- ▶ <command>
- ▶ <datalist>
- ▶ <details>
- ▶ <embed>
- ▶ <figcaption>
- ▶ <figure>
- ▶ <footer>
- ▶ <header>
- ▶ <hgroup>
- ▶ <keygen>
- ▶ <mark>
- ▶ <meter>
- ▶ <nav>
- ▶ <output>
- ▶ <progress>
- ▶ <rp>
- ▶ <rt>

- ▶ <ruby>
- ▶ <section>
- ▶ <source>
- ▶ <summary>
- ▶ <time>
- ▶ <video>

And these are elements that are dropped in HTML5:

- ▶ <acronym>
- ▶ <applet>
- ▶ <basefont>
- ▶ <big>
- ▶ <center>
- ▶ <dir>
- ▶ <font>
- ▶ <frame>
- ▶ <frameset>
- ▶ <isindex>
- ▶ <noframes>
- ▶ <s>
- ▶ <strike>
- ▶ <tt>
- ▶ <u>

LESSON 2

Drawing with the Canvas Element

The HTML5 Canvas element is a popular one, used to display graphics. The element itself is created very simply in HTML5, like this:

```
<canvas height-"yyy" width=xxx">
</canvas>
```

That's all you need to create a Canvas element. So how do you draw graphics in such an element? You use JavaScript, as we'll see in this lesson.

The Canvas element can draw lines, arcs, complex shapes, images, text, and more. Let's jump in to this element now.

Welcome to the Canvas Element

Technically speaking, the Canvas element is very simple in HTML5. Here's the specification:

Element: <canvas>

Start tag required: Yes

End tag required: Yes

Required attributes: Height, width

Supported browsers: Chrome, Firefox, Opera, Safari

The real story takes place in JavaScript with this element, and it will let us draw in the Canvas element example that we'll develop in this lesson, as shown in Figure 2.1.

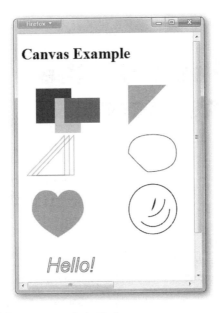

FIGURE 2.1   A Canvas example in Firefox.

Because you use JavaScript to make this element work, we'll look at an overview of what's available first before getting into the details.

Getting to Know the Canvas API

The W3C has created an application programming interface (API) for the Canvas element, specifying the names of the built-in functions and how you use them.

You can find the full Canvas API at http://dev.w3.org/html5/canvas-api/ canvas-2d-api.html. We'll list the most important functions here.

In W3C API specifications, both attributes of the element (these are attributes of the element you use in JavaScript, not in HTML, like this: canvas1.fillStyle = *xxxx*) and the supported JavaScript functions are listed. So you set some aspect of the Canvas with attributes first, then perform some drawing operation like this, where we first set the drawing style with the fillStyle attribute, and then draw a filled rectangle with the fillRect function:

```
canvas1.fillStyle =xxxx
canvas1.fillRect(xx, xx, xx, xx;
```

Each item in the API is prefixed with its types, such as float for floating point number. Here are some representative types you'll see in the W3C specifications:

▶ any For attributes—This means that the attribute can be of any type.

▶ DOMString Means DOM (Document Object Model) String—For our purposes, this is just a quoted text string.

▶ float—This is a floating point number.

Now let's take a look at what the Canvas API lists for attributes and functions.

Styling

You use two attributes for setting drawing style in a Canvas—whether drawing actions should fill in the figure or not:

▶ attribute any fillStyle; // (default black)

▶ attribute any strokeStyle; // (default black)

Setting Line Styles

You can set the line styles the Canvas element will use with these JavaScript attributes:

▶ attribute DOMString lineCap; // "butt", "round", "square" (default "butt")

▶ attribute DOMString lineJoin; // "miter", "round", "bevel"* (default "miter")

▶ attribute float lineWidth; // (default 1)

▶ attribute float miterLimit; // (default 10)

Casting Shadows

The Canvas element even lets you add shadows to your graphics with these attributes:

- ▶ attribute float shadowBlur; // (default 0)
- ▶ attribute DOMString shadowColor; // (default transparent black)
- ▶ attribute float shadowOffsetX; // (default 0)
- ▶ attribute float shadowOffsetY; // (default 0)

Drawing Rectangles

Here are the functions you use for rectangles:

- ▶ clearRect(float x, float y, float w, float h);
- ▶ fillRect(float x, float y, float w, float h);
- ▶ strokeRect(float x, float y, float w, float h);

Drawing Complex Shapes

With the Canvas element, you can draw arcs, Bezier curves, and more using these functions:

- ▶ arc(float x, float y, float radius, float startAngle, float endAngle, boolean anticlockwise);
- ▶ arcTo(float x1, float y1, float x2, float y2, float radius);
- ▶ beginPath();
- ▶ bezierCurveTo(float cp1x, float cp1y, float cp2x, float cp2y, float x, float y);
- ▶ clip();
- ▶ closePath();
- ▶ fill();

- lineTo(float x, float y);
- moveTo(float x, float y);
- quadraticCurveTo(float cpx, float cpy, float x, float y);
- rect(float x, float y, float w, float h);
- stroke();
- boolean isPointInPath(float x, float y);

Drawing Some Text

You can also write text in a Canvas using these attributes and functions:

- attribute DOMString font; // (default 10px sans-serif)
- attribute DOMString textAlign; // "start", "end", "left", "right", "center" (default: "start")
- attribute DOMString textBaseline; // "top", "hanging", "middle", "alphabetic", "ideographic", "bottom" (default: "alphabetic")
- fillText(DOMString text, float x, float y, optional float maxWidth);
- TextMetrics measureText(DOMString text);
- strokeText(DOMString text, float x, float y, optional float maxWidth);

Drawing Images

You can draw images with these functions:

- drawImage(HTMLImageElement image, float dx, float dy, optional float dw, float dh);
- drawImage(HTMLImageElement image, float sx, float sy, float sw, float sh, float dx, float dy, float dw, float dh);
- drawImage(HTMLCanvasElement image, float dx, float dy, optional float dw, float dh);

▶ drawImage(HTMLCanvasElement image, float sx, float sy, float sw, float sh, float dx, float dy, float dw, float dh);

▶ drawImage(HTMLVideoElement image, float dx, float dy, optional float dw, float dh);

▶ drawImage(HTMLVideoElement image, float sx, float sy, float sw, float sh, float dx, float dy, float dw, float dh);

Using Transformations

You can rotate, resize (scale), or move (translate) graphics with these functions:

▶ rotate(float angle);

▶ scale(float x, float y);

▶ translate(float x, float y);

That's the overview of the Canvas API. Now let's put it to work with an example, starting in the next task.

Starting the Canvas Example

To show how to put the Canvas element to work, we're going to create an example named canvas.html, which you can see running in Firefox in Figure 2.1, and whose code appears in its entirety at the end of this lesson.

To get started with the canvas.html example, follow these steps:

1. Create canvas.html using a text editor such as Windows WordPad.

2. Enter the following code to create the <canvas> element and to set up the JavaScript. Note that we're going to put our JavaScript in a function named loader, which is run only after the Canvas element is fully loaded by the browser (don't enter the three vertical dots—they're just there to show that more code is coming).

```
<!DOCTYPE html>
<html>
  <head>
```

```
<title>
  Canvas Example
</title>

<script type="text/javascript">
  function loader()
  {
    .
    .
    .
  </script>
</head>

<body onload="loader()">
  <h1>Canvas Example</h1>
  <canvas id="canvas" width="600"
    height="500">
  </canvas>

</body>
</html>
```

3. Add the JavaScript to create an object corresponding to the Canvas element as shown. We'll use this object to access the Canvas element in JavaScript.

```
<!DOCTYPE html>
<html>
  <head>
    <title>
      Canvas Example
    </title>

    <script type="text/javascript">
      function loader()
      {
      var canvas = document.getElementById
        ('canvas');
      var canvas1 = canvas.getContext('2d');    .
        .
        .
    </script>
  </head>

<body onload="loader()">
  <h1>Canvas Example</h1>
```

```
<canvas id="canvas" width="600"
  height="500">
</canvas>

</body>
</html>
```

4. Save canvas.html. Make sure you save this code in text format. The default format for WordPad, for example, is RTF, rich-text format, which won't work with browsers.

Now we've got our example started. The next thing we'll do is draw some rectangles.

Drawing Rectangles

You can draw hollow rectangles with the strokeRect function:

▶ strokeRect(float x, float y, float w, float h);

Or you can draw filled-in rectangles with the fillRect function:

▶ fillRect(float x, float y, float w, float h);

You pass these functions the (v, y) coordinate of the upper-left corner of the rectangle and the width and height of the rectangle you want. Note that in a Canvas element, the upper-left corner of the Canvas corresponds to (0, 0), positive x is to the left, positive y is downward, and all measurements are in pixels.

In this task, we'll look at the fillRect function. You can set the fill color with the fillStyle attribute. You set this attribute to a color, which you can specify with the rgba() function. You pass the rgba() function four values: the red, green, and blue values (0–255) of the color you're creating, and a visibility factor (0–1, where 0 means the rectangle will be invisible, and 1 means it will be fully visible).

For example, to set the fill style of the canvas1 object to blue, you use this line of code:

▶ canvas1.fillStyle = "rgba(0, 0, 200, 1)";

Here's how to draw multiple rectangles in different colors:

1. Open canvas.html using a text editor such as Windows WordPad.

2. Add the following code to create three rectangles with different fill colors:

```
<script type="text/javascript">
  function loader()
  {
  var canvas = document.getElementById
    ('canvas');
  var canvas1 = canvas.getContext('2d');

  // Rectangles
  canvas1.fillStyle = "rgba(0, 0, 200, 1)";
  canvas1.fillRect(30, 30, 75, 70);

  canvas1.fillStyle = "rgba(200, 200, 0, 1)";
  canvas1.fillRect(70, 50, 55, 70);

  canvas1.fillStyle = "rgba(200, 0, 0, 1)";
  canvas1.fillRect(90, 50, 75, 50);
    .
    .
    .
  }
```

3. Save canvas.html. Make sure you save this code in text format.

You can see the results in Figure 2.2, where all three overlapping rectangles appear.

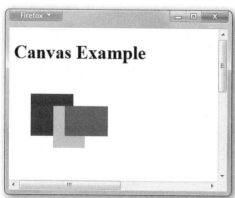

FIGURE 2.2   Drawing rectangles.

Drawing Line Art

You can draw line art using a Canvas control. You start with the beginPath() function to let the Canvas know that you're creating a figure, then use a combination of the moveTo() and lineTo() functions to position the drawing location and actually draw lines.

When your figure is complete, you use the closePath() function to complete the path you've drawn, and use the stroke function to draw the result.

We'll take a look at an example here, where we draw three triangles using these techniques. As an added feature, we'll draw the triangles in red by setting the Canvas's strokeStyle attribute to red:

▸ canvas1.strokeStyle = "rgba(200, 0, 0, 0.5)";

Here's how to draw the triangles:

1. Open canvas.html using a text editor such as Windows WordPad.

2. Add the following code to create three triangles:

```
<script type="text/javascript">
function loader()
{
var canvas = document.getElementById
  ('canvas');
var canvas1 = canvas.getContext('2d');
    .
    .
    .
// Stroked triangles
canvas1.beginPath();
canvas1.strokeStyle = "rgba(200, 0, 0, 0.5)";
canvas1.moveTo(110, 205);
canvas1.lineTo(110, 125);
canvas1.lineTo(30, 205);
canvas1.closePath();
canvas1.stroke();
```

```
canvas1.beginPath();
canvas1.moveTo(100, 205);
canvas1.lineTo(100, 125);
canvas1.lineTo(20, 205);
canvas1.closePath();
canvas1.stroke();

canvas1.beginPath();
canvas1.moveTo(90, 205);
canvas1.lineTo(90, 125);
canvas1.lineTo(10, 205);
canvas1.closePath();
canvas1.stroke();
```

3. Save canvas.html. Make sure you save this code in text format.

You can see the results in Figure 2.3, where all three overlapping triangles appear.

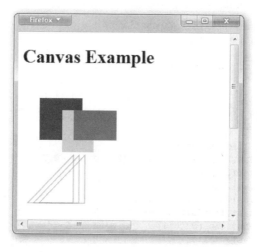

FIGURE 2.3 Drawing triangles.

Filling Line Art

You can also fill in the figures you draw with color. For example, here we'll see how to draw a solid green triangle.

In this case, you draw the triangle much like you did in the previous task—using beginPath(), moveTo(), lineTo(), and closePath(). But when it's time to draw the triangle, you use the fill() function, not the stroke() function.

The fill() function fills a figure with the canvas's current fill color, which you set with the fillStyle attribute. For example, here's how we set the fill color to light green:

▶ canvas1.fillStyle = "rgba(0, 200, 0, 0.5)";

Here's how to draw the entire green triangle:

1. Open canvas.html using a text editor such as Windows WordPad.

2. Add the following code to create the green triangle:

```
<script type="text/javascript">
function loader()
{
var canvas = document.getElementById
  ('canvas');
var canvas1 = canvas.getContext('2d');
  .
  .
  .
//Filled triangle
canvas1.fillStyle = "rgba(0, 200, 0, 0.5)";
canvas1.beginPath();
canvas1.moveTo(225, 25);
canvas1.lineTo(305, 25);
canvas1.lineTo(225, 105);
canvas1.closePath();
canvas1.fill();
```

3. Save canvas.html. Make sure you save this code in text format.

You can see the results in Figure 2.4, where the filled triangle appears.

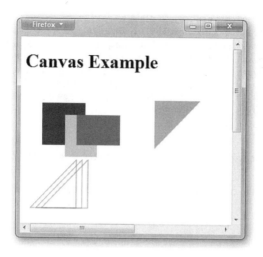

FIGURE 2.4   Drawing a filled triangle.

Drawing with Bezier Curves

You're not limited to drawing lines using lineTo. You can also draw Bezier curves with the bezierCurveTo() function:

> ▶ bezierCurveTo(float cp1x, float cp1y, float cp2x, float cp2y, float x, float y);

Here's an example that draws a red heart using Bezier curves:

1. Open canvas.html using a text editor such as Windows WordPad.

2. Add the following code to create the filled heart:

```
<script type="text/javascript">
  function loader()
  {
  var canvas = document.getElementById
    ('canvas');
  var canvas1 = canvas.getContext('2d');
    .
    .
    .
  // Heart
  canvas1.fillStyle = "rgba(200, 0, 0, 0.5)";
  canvas1.beginPath();
```

```
canvas1.moveTo(75, 250);
canvas1.bezierCurveTo(75, 247, 70, 235, 50, 235);
canvas1.bezierCurveTo(20, 235, 20, 272.5, 20, 272);
canvas1.bezierCurveTo(20, 290, 40, 312, 75, 330);
canvas1.bezierCurveTo(110, 312, 130, 290, 130, 272);
canvas1.bezierCurveTo(130, 272.5, 130, 235, 100, 235);
canvas1.bezierCurveTo(85, 235, 75, 247, 75, 250);
canvas1.closePath();
canvas1.fill();
```

3. Save canvas.html. Make sure you save this code in text format.

You can see the results in Figure 2.5, where the red heart appears.

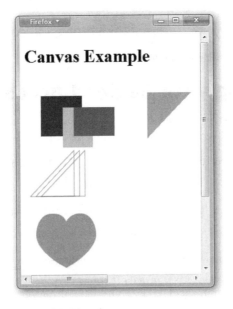

FIGURE 2.5   Drawing a filled heart.

Drawing with Quadratic Curves

Besides the Bezier curves you saw in the previous task, you can also draw with quadratic curves by using the quadraticCurveTo() function:

▶ quadraticCurveTo(float cpx, float cpy, float x, float y);

Here's an example that draws a shape using quadratic curves:

1. Open canvas.html using a text editor such as Windows WordPad.

2. Add the following code to create the quadratic curve figure:

```
<script type="text/javascript">
function loader()
{
var canvas = document.getElementById
  ('canvas');
var canvas1 = canvas.getContext('2d');
.
.
.
//Quadratic curves
canvas1.strokeStyle = "rgba(0, 0, 0, 1)";
canvas1.beginPath();
canvas1.moveTo(275, 125);
canvas1.quadraticCurveTo(225, 125, 225, 162);
canvas1.quadraticCurveTo(260, 200, 265, 200);
canvas1.quadraticCurveTo(325, 200, 325, 162);
canvas1.quadraticCurveTo(325, 125, 275, 125);
canvas1.closePath();
canvas1.stroke();
```

3. Save canvas.html. Make sure you save this code in text format.

You can see the results in Figure 2.6, where the shape drawn with quadratic curves appears.

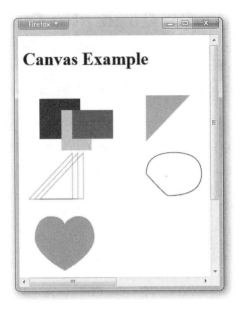

FIGURE 2.6   Drawing with quadratic curves.

Drawing Arcs

The canvas control can also draw arcs with the arc function:

▶ arc(float x, float y, float radius, float startAngle, float endAngle, boolean anticlockwise);

Here's an example that draws a shape using quadratic curves:

1. Open canvas.html using a text editor such as Windows WordPad.

2. Add the following code to create the arcs (note the use of the JavaScript constant Math.PI to get the value of pi):

```
<script type="text/javascript">
  function loader()
  {
  var canvas = document.getElementById
    ('canvas');
  var canvas1 = canvas.getContext('2d');
    .
```

```
    .
    .
// Arcs
canvas1.beginPath();
canvas1.arc(275, 275, 50, 0, Math.PI * 2, true);

canvas1.moveTo(310, 275);
canvas1.arc(275, 275, 35, 0, 0.75 * Math.PI, false);

canvas1.moveTo(300, 255);
canvas1.arc(265, 255, 35, 0, 0.5 * Math.PI, false);

canvas1.moveTo(280, 255);
canvas1.arc(245, 255, 35, 0, 0.2 * Math.PI, false);
canvas1.closePath();
canvas1.stroke();
```

3. Save canvas.html. Make sure you save this code in text format.

You can see the results in Figure 2.7, where you can see the arcs.

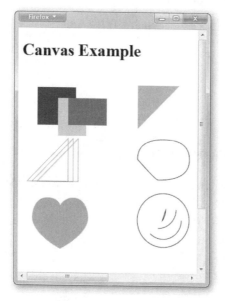

FIGURE 2.7 Drawing with arcs.

Drawing Text

You can draw text as well in the Canvas control. To do that, start by selecting a font to use by setting the Canvas control's font attribute to a string that contains the specification for the font you select, like this:

▶ canvas1.font = 'italic 40px sans-serif';

This line of JavaScript installs the italic san-serif font that is 40 pixels high as the default font (if you don't want italics, just omit "italic").

After setting the font you want, you can draw text with a function like strokeText(), which you pass the text you want to draw and that text's position, as we'll do in this example:

1. Open canvas.html using a text editor such as Windows WordPad.

2. Add the following code to draw text:

```
<script type="text/javascript">
function loader()
{
var canvas = document.getElementById
  ('canvas');
var canvas1 = canvas.getContext('2d');
    .
    .
    .
canvas1.font = 'italic 40px sans-serif';
canvas1.strokeText("Hello!", 50, 400);
```

3. Save canvas.html. Make sure you save this code in text format.

You can see the results in Figure 2.8, where you can see the text at the bottom of the figure.

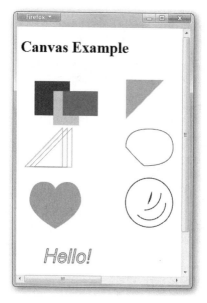

FIGURE 2.8   Drawing text.

The canvas.html Example Code

Here's the full code of the canvas.html example that we developed in this lesson for reference:

```
<!DOCTYPE html>
<html>
  <head>
    <title>
      Canvas Example
    </title>

    <script type="text/javascript">
      function loader()
      {
      var canvas = document.getElementById
        ('canvas');
      var canvas1 = canvas.getContext('2d');

      // Rectangles
      canvas1.fillStyle = "rgba(0, 0, 200, 1)";
      canvas1.fillRect(30, 30, 75, 70);
```

```
canvas1.fillStyle = "rgba(200, 200, 0, 1)";
canvas1.fillRect(70, 50, 55, 70);

canvas1.fillStyle = "rgba(200, 0, 0, 1)";
canvas1.fillRect(90, 50, 75, 50);

//Filled triangle
canvas1.fillStyle = "rgba(0, 200, 0, 0.5)";
canvas1.beginPath();
canvas1.moveTo(225, 25);
canvas1.lineTo(305, 25);
canvas1.lineTo(225, 105);
canvas1.closePath();
canvas1.fill();

// Stroked triangles
canvas1.beginPath();
canvas1.strokeStyle = "rgba(200, 0, 0, 0.5)";
canvas1.moveTo(110, 205);
canvas1.lineTo(110, 125);
canvas1.lineTo(30, 205);
canvas1.closePath();
canvas1.stroke();

canvas1.beginPath();
canvas1.moveTo(100, 205);
canvas1.lineTo(100, 125);
canvas1.lineTo(20, 205);
canvas1.closePath();
canvas1.stroke();

canvas1.beginPath();
canvas1.moveTo(90, 205);
canvas1.lineTo(90, 125);
canvas1.lineTo(10, 205);
canvas1.closePath();
canvas1.stroke();

// Heart
canvas1.fillStyle = "rgba(200, 0, 0, 0.5)";
canvas1.beginPath();
canvas1.moveTo(75, 250);
canvas1.bezierCurveTo(75, 247, 70, 235, 50, 235);
canvas1.bezierCurveTo(20, 235, 20, 272.5, 20, 272);
canvas1.bezierCurveTo(20, 290, 40, 312, 75, 330);
```

```
canvas1.bezierCurveTo(110, 312, 130, 290, 130, 272);
canvas1.bezierCurveTo(130, 272.5, 130, 235, 100, 235);
canvas1.bezierCurveTo(85, 235, 75, 247, 75, 250);
canvas1.closePath();
canvas1.fill();

//Quadratic curves
canvas1.strokeStyle = "rgba(0, 0, 0, 1)";
canvas1.beginPath();
canvas1.moveTo(275, 125);
canvas1.quadraticCurveTo(225, 125, 225, 162);
canvas1.quadraticCurveTo(260, 200, 265, 200);
canvas1.quadraticCurveTo(325, 200, 325, 162);
canvas1.quadraticCurveTo(325, 125, 275, 125);
canvas1.closePath();
canvas1.stroke();

// Arcs
canvas1.beginPath();
canvas1.arc(275, 275, 50, 0, Math.PI * 2, true);

canvas1.moveTo(310, 275);
canvas1.arc(275, 275, 35, 0, 0.75 * Math.PI, false);

canvas1.moveTo(300, 255);
canvas1.arc(265, 255, 35, 0, 0.5 * Math.PI, false);

canvas1.moveTo(280, 255);
canvas1.arc(245, 255, 35, 0, 0.2 * Math.PI, false);
canvas1.closePath();

canvas1.stroke();

canvas1.font = 'italic 40px sans-serif';
canvas1.strokeText("Hello!", 50, 400);          }
</script>
</head>

<body onload="loader()">
  <h1>Canvas Example</h1>
  <canvas id="canvas" width="600"
    height="500">
  </canvas>

</body>
</html>
```

LESSON 3

Dragging and Dropping with HTML5

HTML5 supports drag-and-drop operations, where you can move elements and text around the browser window using a mouse or other pointing device.

That's useful for such operations as letting the user move items into a shopping cart, or letting them customize what elements appear in their home page, and it's a very popular part of HTML5.

Drag and drop is supported by a number of attributes added to HTML5 elements, such as the draggable attribute, which you set to true to make the element draggable. However, you do most of the work supporting drag and drop yourself, in a scripting language, such as JavaScript, as you'll see.

Let's jump into drag and drop operations immediately.

Welcome to Drag and Drop

From the point of view of HTML5 elements, drag and drop is pretty simple, involving these element attributes:

- ▶ Required attributes: draggable, ondragenter, ondragover, ondrop, ondragstart, ondragend

- ▶ Supported browsers: Chrome, Firefox, Opera, Safari

The real story takes place in scripting languages such as JavaScript, as you'll see. You connect each of the "on" attributes, such as ondragstart, to a JavaScript function like this for ondragstart, which occurs when the user starts dragging a draggable element:

```
ondragstart = "return start(event)";
```

It's up to you to write the code for the JavaScript function you connect to each of the "on" attributes.

TIP: Note that all the "on" attributes start with "ondrag" with one exception—ondrop, which occurs when you drop a dragged item. It's worth bearing in mind that this attribute is ondrop, not ondrag-drop, or you're going to confuse some browsers, which will not run your code.

In this lesson, we'll create the drag-and-drop example, draganddrop.html, you see in Figures 3.1 and 3.2. There are three <div> elements that you can drag around, labeled 1, 2, and 3. We've set up the example so that not all <div> elements can be dropped on the large square targets in the page. For example, if you try to drop <div> 1 onto the second target, you'll just get a "no" symbol, as shown in Figure 3.1, that indicates that target won't accept <div> 1. On the other hand, you can drop <div> 1 onto the third target, as shown in Figure 3.2.

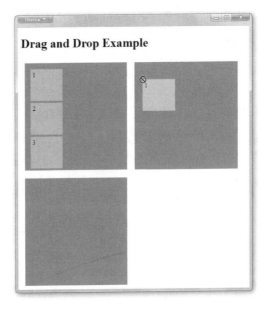

FIGURE 3.1   Denying a drag-and-drop operation.

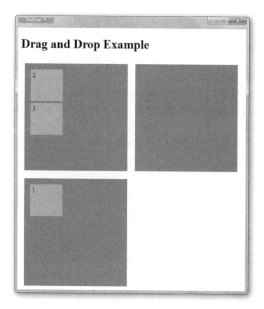

FIGURE 3.2   Allowing a drag-and-drop operation.

Now let's take a look at the draggable attribute and the "on" attributes and how you use them to support drag and drop.

Getting to Know the Drag-and-Drop API

You can read all about the drag-and-drop specification according to the W3C at: http://dev.w3.org/html5/spec/dnd.html.

From an HTML point of view, drag and drop is supported with these attributes:

- ▶ draggable
- ▶ ondragenter
- ▶ ondragover
- ▶ ondrop

▶ ondragstart

▶ ondragend

The draggable attribute of an element, as you might guess, is set to true if you want to allow that element to be dragged. The "on" attributes are used to connect JavaScript functions to various events. For example, you use ondragenter to call a JavaScript function when a draggable element is being dragged over another element (and in the JavaScript function, you can indicate to the browser whether you can drop the draggable item there).

Let's take a look at each of these attributes briefly; then we'll put them to work in the draganddrop.html example.

The draggable Attribute

The draggable attribute is the most basic of all drag-and-drop attributes. To make an element draggable, you set its draggable attribute to true:

```
<div id="draggable3" draggable="true">
</div>
```

Doing so informs the browser that this element can be dragged, but setting this attribute isn't all that's needed—you also have to connect up JavaScript functions to the "on" attributes to make this work.

The ondragenter Attribute

Drag enter events occur in a drop target when the user drags a draggable element over that target.

You can connect this event to a JavaScript handler function (which it's up to you to write) like this:

```
<div id="target1"
  ondragenter="return enter(event)"
    .
    .
    .
```

Note that this event occurs in drop targets, not in draggable elements.

The ondragover Attribute

Dragover events occur in a drop target while users drag a draggable element over that target. You can connect this event to a JavaScript handler function like this:

```
<div id="target1"
  ondragenter="return enter(event)"
  ondragover="return over(event)"
  .
  .
  .
```

This event occurs in drop targets.

The ondrop Attribute

Drop events occur in a drop target while users drop a draggable element onto that target. You can connect this event to a JavaScript handler function like this:

```
<div id="target1"
  ondragenter="return enter(event)"
  ondragover="return over(event)"
  ondrop="return drop(event)">
```

This event occurs in drop targets; note that it's ondrop, not ondragdrop!

The ondragstart Attribute

This event occurs in draggable elements when users start dragging them. You can connect JavaScript function handlers to this event like this:

```
<div id="draggable1" draggable="true"
  ondragstart="return start(event)"
  .
  .
  .
```

This event occurs in draggable elements.

The ondragend Attribute

This event occurs in draggable elements when users stop dragging them.
You can connect JavaScript function handlers to this event like this:

```
<div id="draggable1" draggable="true"
  ondragstart="return start(event)"
  ondragend="return end(event)">1
.
.
.
```

This event occurs in draggable elements.

The dataTransfer Object

There is one more item you should know about—the dataTransfer that
comes built in to event objects in HTML5—because it offers support for
drag-and-drop operations. You access this object through the event object
passed to you when drag-and-drop operations start.

For example, the dataTransfer object has a property named effectAllowed
that lets you specify what drag-and-drop operation is allowed. It has functions named setData() and getData() to allow you to specify what data you
want to drag and drop with a draggable element, and another function
named setDragImage() lets you specify the image of the item being
dragged.

Here's how using dataTransfer in JavaScript might work, where we're
specifying that move operations are OK, storing the ID of the draggable
element so we know what element to move when the drag operation is
complete, and setting the image that the user drags to be a copy of the
draggable element that the mouse clicked (as given by the event object e's
target attribute):

```
e.dataTransfer.effectAllowed='move';
e.dataTransfer.setData("Data",
  e.target.getAttribute('id'));
e.dataTransfer.setDragImage(e.target, 0, 0);
```

To make this clear, let's see all this at work in an example.

Starting the Drag-and-Drop Example

To show how to put drag and drop to work, we're going to create an example named draganddrop.html, which you can see running in Figures 3.1 and 3.2, and whose code appears in its entirety at the end of this lesson.

To get started with the draganddrop.html example, follow these steps:

1. Create draganddrop.html using a text editor such as Windows WordPad.

2. Enter the following code to create the three targets onto which draggable elements can be dropped. Note that we will use <div> elements for the targets and that we connect the drag-and-drop events that targets support to JavaScript functions that we will write later.

```
<!DOCTYPE HTML>
<html>
  <head>
    <title>
      Drag and Drop Example
    </title>
  </head>

  <body>
    <h1>Drag and Drop Example</h1>

    <div id="target1"
      ondragenter="return enter(event)"
      ondragover="return over(event)"
      ondrop="return drop(event)">
    </div>

    <div id="target2"
      ondragenter="return enter(event)"
      ondragover="return over(event)"
      ondrop="return drop(event)">
    </div>

    <div id="target3"
      ondragenter="return enter(event)"
      ondragover="return over(event)"
```

```
    ondrop="return drop(event)">
    </div>
  </body>
</html>
```

3. Add the following code to create the three draggable <div> elements as children of the first target. Note that we set each draggable <div> element's draggable attribute to true and also connect the events that draggables support to JavaScript functions, which we will write later.

```
<!DOCTYPE HTML>
<html>
  <head>
    <title>
      Drag and Drop Example
    </title>
  </head>

  <body>
    <h1>Drag and Drop Example</h1>

    <div id="target1"
      ondragenter="return enter(event)"
      ondragover="return over(event)"
      ondrop="return drop(event)">

      <div id="draggable1" draggable="true"
        ondragstart="return start(event)"
        ondragend="return end(event)">1
      </div>

      <div id="draggable2" draggable="true"
        ondragstart="return start(event)"
        ondragend="return end(event)">2
      </div>

      <div id="draggable3" draggable="true"
        ondragstart="return start(event)"
        ondragend="return end(event)">3
      </div>
    </div>

    <div id="target2"
      ondragenter="return enter(event)"
      ondragover="return over(event)"
      ondrop="return drop(event)">
    </div>
```

```
<div id="target3"
  ondragenter="return enter(event)"
  ondragover="return over(event)"
  ondrop="return drop(event)">
</div>
</body>
</html>
```

4. Save draganddrop.html. Make sure you save this code in text format (the default format for WordPad, for example, is RTF, rich-text format, which won't work with browsers).

Now we've got our example started with the three targets and three draggable elements. All that is invisible so far, however, so we will style them next.

Styling the Draggable and Target Elements

In this task, we'll make the <div> elements we use for the targets and draggables visible. In particular, we'll style the targets in cyan and the draggables in orange.

To do so, follow these steps:

1. Open draganddrop.html using a text editor such as Windows WordPad.

2. Add the following code to style the draggable <div> elements and the target <div> elements, as well as give them a size.

```
<!DOCTYPE HTML>
<html>
  <head>
    <title>
      Drag and Drop Example
    </title>

    <style type="text/css">
      #target1, #target2, #target3
      {
```

```
            float:left; width:250px; height:250px;
            padding:10px; margin:10px;
        }

        #draggable1, #draggable2, #draggable3
        {
            width:75px; height:70px; padding:5px;
            margin:5px;
        }

        #target1 {background-color: cyan;}
        #target2 {background-color: cyan;}
        #target3 {background-color: cyan;}

        #draggable1 {background-color: orange;}
        #draggable2 {background-color: orange;}
        #draggable3 {background-color: orange;}
    </style>

</head>

<body>
    <h1>Drag and Drop Example</h1>

    <div id="target1"
        ondragenter="return enter(event)"
        ondragover="return over(event)"
        ondrop="return drop(event)">

        <div id="draggable1" draggable="true"
            ondragstart="return start(event)"
            ondragend="return end(event)">1
        </div>

        <div id="draggable2" draggable="true"
            ondragstart="return start(event)"
            ondragend="return end(event)">2
        </div>

        <div id="draggable3" draggable="true"
            ondragstart="return start(event)"
            ondragend="return end(event)">3
        </div>
    </div>

    <div id="target2"
        ondragenter="return enter(event)"
```

```
      ondragover="return over(event)"
      ondrop="return drop(event)">
   </div>

   <div id="target3"
      ondragenter="return enter(event)"
      ondragover="return over(event)"
      ondrop="return drop(event)">
   </div>
</body>
</html>
```

3. Save draganddrop.html. Make sure you save this code in text format (the default format for WordPad, for example, is RTF, rich-text format, which won't work with browsers).

Now you can see the draggables and the targets as shown in Figure 3.3.

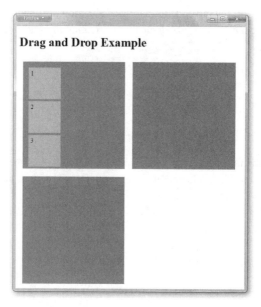

FIGURE 3.3   The draggables and targets in draganddrop.html.

Starting the Drag Operation

When the user starts dragging a draggable <div> element in our example, that <div> element's ondragstart event occurs, and we've tied that event to a JavaScript function named start().

In this task, we'll write the start() function to get the dragging operation started. That involves three steps: setting the allowed drag operation to "move" so the draggable <div> element that the user wants to drag may be dragged, storing the ID of the element that's being dragged so we can move it when it's dropped, and setting the image that the user will drag around.

To do all these things, follow these steps:

1. Open draganddrop.html using a text editor such as Windows WordPad.

2. Add the following code to the <head> section of dragdrop.html, starting a new <script> element, and creating the start() function:

```
<script type="text/javascript">
  function start(e)
  {
    .
    .
    .
  }
```

3. Add the following code to the start() function to indicate that the draggable <div> element the user is attempting to drag may indeed be moved (which you do by setting the dataTransfer.effectAllowed property of the event object passed to the start() function to "move"):

```
<script type="text/javascript">
  function start(e)
  {
    e.dataTransfer.effectAllowed='move';
    .
    .
    .
  }
```

4. Add the following code to the start() function to store the ID of the <div> element being dragged so we can move it when it's dropped:

```
<script type="text/javascript">
  function start(e)
  {
    e.dataTransfer.effectAllowed='move';
    e.dataTransfer.setData("Data",
      e.target.getAttribute('id'));
    .
    .
    .
  }
```

5. Add the following code to the start() function to set the drag image to the draggable <div> element, with an offset of (0, 0):

```
<script type="text/javascript">
  function start(e)
  {
    e.dataTransfer.effectAllowed='move';
    e.dataTransfer.setData("Data",
      e.target.getAttribute('id'));
    e.dataTransfer.setDragImage(e.target, 0, 0);
    return true;
  }
```

6. Save draganddrop.html. Make sure you save this code in text format (the default format for WordPad, for example, is RTF, rich-text format, which won't work with browsers).

Now the user will be able to drag the draggable <div> elements in this example.

Allowing Dragged Objects to Enter the Targets

When the user drags a draggable <div> element to a target <div> element, the target <div> element's ondragEnter event occurs. We've tied that event to a JavaScript function named enter(), and in that function, we want to indicate that draggable objects are allowed to enter the target by returning a value of true from the enter() function.

To do that, follow these steps:

1. Open draganddrop.html using a text editor such as Windows WordPad.

2. Add the following code to the <script> section of dragdrop.html, creating the enter() function and returning a value of true from it, indicating that draggable elements may enter a target:

```
function enter(e)
{
  return true;
}
```

3. Save draganddrop.html. Make sure you save this code in text format (the default format for WordPad, for example, is RTF, rich-text format, which won't work with browsers).

Now the user will be able to drag the draggable <div> elements to the targets.

Allowing Dragged Objects to Be Dropped on Certain Targets

When the user drags a draggable <div> element over a target, that target's ondragover event occurs, and we've tied that event to a function named over(). You can use the over() function to indicate whether the dragged item may be dropped on the current target. If you return a value of true from this function, the dragged item may not be dropped; returning a value of false means that it can be dropped.

To create the over() function, follow these steps:

1. Open draganddrop.html using a text editor such as Windows WordPad.

2. Add the following code to the <script> section of dragdrop.html, creating the over() function and getting the ID of the dragged item (iddraggable) and the ID of the target (id):

```
function over(e)
{
  var iddraggable =
```

```
    e.dataTransfer.getData("Data");
    var id = e.target.getAttribute('id');
    .
    .
    .
}
```

3. Add the following code to the over() function to indicate that any dragged item may be dropped on target 1, that draggable <div> element 3 may be dropped on target 2 only, and that draggable <div> elements 1 and 2 may be dropped on target 3 only:

```
function over(e)
{
  var iddraggable =
    e.dataTransfer.getData("Data");
  var id = e.target.getAttribute('id');

  if(id =='target1')
    return false;

  if((id =='target2')
    && iddraggable == 'draggable3')
    return false;

  else if(id =='target3'
    && (iddraggable == 'draggable1' ||
    iddraggable =='draggable2'))
    return false;

  else
    return true;
}
```

4. Save draganddrop.html. Make sure you save this code in text format (the default format for WordPad, for example, is RTF, rich-text format, which won't work with browsers).

Now you've indicated to the browser which draggable <div> elements may be dropped on which target <div> elements.

Handling Drop Events

When the user drops a draggable <div> element on an allowed target <div> element, how do we move the draggable <div> to the target? That turns out to be simple—we'll just use the built-in JavaScript function appendChild to append the draggable <div> element to the current target <div> element.

When the user drops a draggable <div> element on a target, the ondrop event occurs in the target element, and we have connected a JavaScript function named drop() to implement the drop operation. To add drop() to the draganddrop.html example, follow these steps:

1. Open draganddrop.html using a text editor such as Windows WordPad.

2. Add the following code to the <script> section of dragdrop.html, creating the drop() function and getting the ID of the dragged item (iddraggable):

```
function drop(e)
{
  var iddraggable =
    e.dataTransfer.getData("Data");
  .
  .
  .
}
```

3. Add the following code to the drop() function to append the draggable <div> element to the target <div> element, as well as stopping further propagation of the event in the browser with the stopPropagation() function (returning a value of false also stops further propagation of the event):

```
function drop(e)
{
  var iddraggable =
    e.dataTransfer.getData("Data");
  e.target.appendChild
    (document.getElementById(iddraggable));
  e.stopPropagation();
  return false;
}
```

4. Save draganddrop.html. Make sure you save this code in text format (the default format for WordPad, for example, is RTF, rich-text format, which won't work with browsers).

Now you've handled the drop operation.

Ending Drop Operations

When a draggable <div> element is dropped, its ondragEnd event occurs, and we've tied that event to the JavaScript function end(). We'll add code to the end() function to clear the data stored in the dataTransfer object (that is, the ID of the element being dragged) now that the drop operation is finished. Just follow these steps:

1. Open draganddrop.html using a text editor such as Windows WordPad.

2. Add the following code to the <script> section of dragdrop.html, creating the end() function and then ending the <script> section in draganddrop.html:

```
function end(e)
{
   e.dataTransfer.clearData("Data");
   return true
}
</script>
```

3. Save draganddrop.html. Make sure you save this code in text format (the default format for WordPad, for example, is RTF, rich-text format, which won't work with browsers).

Now you've completed the draganddrop.html example and can drag and drop using any supported browser, as shown in Figure 3.4.

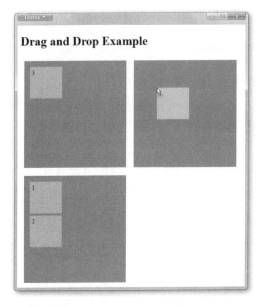

FIGURE 3.4   Dragging and dropping with draganddrop.html.

The draganddrop.html Example Code

Here's the full code of the draganddrop.html example that we developed in this lesson for reference:

```
<!DOCTYPE HTML>
<html>
  <head>
    <title>
      Drag and Drop Example
    </title>

    <style type="text/css">
      #target1, #target2, #target3
      {
        float:left; width:250px; height:250px;
        padding:10px; margin:10px;
      }
```

```
#draggable1, #draggable2, #draggable3
{
    width:75px; height:70px; padding:5px;
    margin:5px;
}

#target1 {background-color: cyan;}
#target2 {background-color: cyan;}
#target3 {background-color: cyan;}

#draggable1 {background-color: orange;}
#draggable2 {background-color: orange;}
#draggable3 {background-color: orange;}
</style>

<script type="text/javascript">
    function start(e)
    {
        e.dataTransfer.effectAllowed='move';
        e.dataTransfer.setData("Data",
          e.target.getAttribute('id'));
        e.dataTransfer.setDragImage(e.target, 0, 0);
        return true;
    }

    function enter(e)
    {
        return true;
    }

    function over(e)
    {
        var iddraggable =
          e.dataTransfer.getData("Data");
        var id = e.target.getAttribute('id');

        if(id =='target1')
          return false;

        if((id =='target2')
            && iddraggable == 'draggable3')
          return false;

        else if(id =='target3'
            && (iddraggable == 'draggable1' ||
```

```
        iddraggable =='draggable2'))
        return false;

      else
        return true;
  }

  function drop(e)
  {
    var iddraggable =
      e.dataTransfer.getData("Data");
    e.target.appendChild
      (document.getElementById(iddraggable));
    e.stopPropagation();
    return false;
  }

  function end(e)
  {
    e.dataTransfer.clearData("Data");
    return true
  }
  </script>
</head>

<body>
  <h1>Drag and Drop Example</h1>

  <div id="target1"
    ondragenter="return enter(event)"
    ondragover="return over(event)"
    ondrop="return drop(event)">

    <div id="draggable1" draggable="true"
      ondragstart="return start(event)"
      ondragend="return end(event)">1
    </div>

    <div id="draggable2" draggable="true"
      ondragstart="return start(event)"
      ondragend="return end(event)">2
    </div>

    <div id="draggable3" draggable="true"
      ondragstart="return start(event)"
      ondragend="return end(event)">3
```

```
      </div>
    </div>

    <div id="target2"
      ondragenter="return enter(event)"
      ondragover="return over(event)"
      ondrop="return drop(event)">
    </div>

    <div id="target3"
      ondragenter="return enter(event)"
      ondragover="return over(event)"
      ondrop="return drop(event)">
    </div>
  </body>
</html>
```

LESSON 4

Web Form Controls

HTML has always supported form controls using the <input> element, such as text boxes:

```
<input name="text" type="text">
```

or radio buttons:

```
<input name="radio" type="radio">
```

You create such controls using the <input> element with the type attribute set to the type of control you want (check box, radio button, text field), and the name attribute set to the name of the control as you'll reference it in code (in a scripting language like JavaScript or a server-side language like PHP).

HTML5 extends the number of form controls available to you, adding such controls as a date-time picker and a numeric range control. Those new controls are the focus of this lesson.

We'll also create an example in this lesson, webforms.html, that displays the new controls. The only browser that displays the new controls so far is the Opera browser, so this example runs in Opera. We'll also create a small PHP server-side program that displays the value you entered into the date time picker control when you click the Submit button in this example to show how you can extract data from these controls on the server (but note that you don't have to know PHP to read this book).

For reference, you can read what W3C has to say about the web form controls at www.whatwg.org/specs/web-apps/current-work/multipage/the-input-element.html#attr-input-type.

Let's jump into web form controls now.

Welcome to Web Form Controls

As mentioned, you create web form controls with the <input> element, setting the type attribute to indicate which control you want:

Element: <input>

Required attributes: You specify which web form control you want with the type attribute.

Supported browsers: Opera

Which controls are available in HTML5? You can see the list by type attribute in HTML5 in Table 4.1 (not all are new to HTML5, of course).

TABLE 4.1   The Web Form Controls

Type	Control Type
button	A button
checkbox	A check box
color	A color well
date	A date control
datetime	A date and time control
datetime-local	A date and time control
email	A text field
file	A label and a button
hidden	n/a
image	Either a clickable image or a button
month	A month control
number	A text field or spinner control
password	Text field that obscures data entry
radio	A radio button
range	A slider control or similar
reset	A button
search	Search field
submit	A button
tel	A text field
text	Text field

TABLE 4.1   The Web Form Controls

Type	Control Type
time	A time control
url	A text field
week	A week control

In this lesson, we're going to create an example named webforms.html that focuses on the new HTML5 controls, as shown in Figure 4.1, running in the Opera browser.

FIGURE 4.1   The webforms.html example.

As a demonstration, we'll also write a small program, webforms.php, in the PHP language, that will run on a server and will read the value entered into the datetime control in webforms.html and report that value, as shown in Figure 4.2. By reading data from a particular control, the PHP script shows how to read data from any web form control on the server, if that's what you want to do.

Now let's get deeper into the web form controls, taking a look at which attributes and function are available.

FIGURE 4.2   Reading the value from a datetime control.

Getting to Know the Web Form Controls API

You know that you create web form controls with the <input> element, setting the type attribute as shown in Table 4.1. But what other attributes are available for each control? For example, when you use a range control—which lets the user specify values using a slider—you can use min and max attributes in the <input> element in addition to the type attribute.

Table 4.2 shows which attributes are allowed with which controls. In addition, each control has built-in functions, which can be called in JavaScript when you access the control as an object, and you'll find those functions in Table 4.3. Finally, many controls have built-in events that occur when the user enters data; you'll find those events in Table 4.4.

TABLE 4.2 Allowed Control Attributes

	Hidden	Text, Search, URL, Telephone	E-mail	Pass-word	Date and Time, Date, Month, Week, Time	Local Date Time	Number	Range	Color	Checkbox, Radio Button	File Upload	Submit Button	Image Button	Reset Button, Button, Button
accept	.	.	.	.	.	.	.	.	.	.	X	.	.	.
alt	.	.	.	.	.	.	.	.	.	.	.	.	X	.
autocomplete	.	X	X	X	X	X	X	X	X	.	.	.	.	.
checked	.	.	.	.	.	.	.	.	.	X	.	.	.	.
formaction	.	.	.	.	.	.	.	.	.	.	.	X	X	.
formenctype	.	.	.	.	.	.	.	.	.	.	.	X	X	.
formmethod	.	.	.	.	.	.	.	.	.	.	.	X	X	.
formnovalidate	.	.	.	.	.	.	.	.	.	.	.	X	X	.
formtarget	.	.	.	.	.	.	.	.	.	.	.	X	X	.
height	.	.	.	.	.	.	.	.	.	.	.	.	X	.

TABLE 4.2 Allowed Control Attributes

	Hidden	Text, Search, URL, Telephone	E-mail	Password	Date and Time, Date, Month, Week, Time	Local Date Time, and Number	Range	Color	Checkbox, Radio Button	File Upload	Submit Button	Image Button	Reset Button
list	·	X	X	·	X	X	X	X	·	·	·	·	·
max	·	·	·	·	X	X	X	·	·	·	·	·	·
maxlength	·	X	X	X	·	·	·	·	·	·	·	·	·
min	·	·	·	·	X	X	X	·	·	·	·	·	·
multiple	·	·	X	·	·	·	·	·	·	X	·	·	·
pattern	·	X	X	X	·	·	·	·	·	·	·	·	·
placeholder	·	X	X	X	·	·	·	·	·	·	·	·	·
readonly	·	X	X	X	X	X	·	·	·	·	·	·	·
required	·	X	X	X	X	X	·	·	X	X	·	·	·
size	·	X	X	X	·	·	·	·	·	·	·	·	·
src	·	·	·	·	·	·	·	·	·	·	·	X	·
step	·	·	·	·	X	X	X	·	·	·	·	·	·
width	·	·	·	·	·	·	·	·	·	·	·	X	·

TABLE 4.3   Built-in Control Data Attributes and Functions

	Hidden	Text, Search, URL, Telephone	E-mail	Password	Date and Time, Local Date, Date, Month, Week, Time	Number	Range	Color	Checkbox, Radio Button	File Upload	Submit Button	Image Button	Reset Button, Button
checked									X				
files										X			
value	default	value	value	value	value	value	value	value	default/on	filename	default	default	default
valueAsDate					X								
valueAsNumber					X	X	X	X					
list		X	X		X	X	X	X					
selectedOption		X	X		X	X	X	X					
select()		X	X	X									
selectionStart		X	X	X									
selectionEnd		X	X	X									
setSelectionRange()		X	X	X									
stepDown()					X	X	X						
stepUp()					X	X	X						

TABLE 4.4 Control Events

	Hidden	Text, Search, URL, Telephone	E-mail	Password	Date and Time, Date, Month, Week, Time	Local Date Time, and Number	Range	Color	Checkbox, Radio Button	File Upload	Submit Button	Image Button	Reset Button
input	·	X	X	X	X	X	X	X	·	·	·	·	·
change	·	X	X	X	X	X	X	X	X	X	·	·	·

Whereas some controls return simple text strings, others return formatted data. You can see the data types returned by each control in Table 4.5.

TABLE 4.5   Control Data Types

Type	Data Type
button	n/a
checkbox	A set of zero or more values from a predefined list
color	An sRGB color with 8-bit red, green, and blue components
date	A date (year, month, day) with no time zone
datetime	A date and time (year, month, day, hour, minute, second, fraction of a second) with the time zone set to UTC
datetime-local	A date and time (year, month, day, hour, minute, second, fraction of a second) with no time zone
email	An email address or list of email addresses
file	Zero or more files each with a MIME type and optionally a filename
hidden	An arbitrary string
image	A coordinate, relative to a particular image's size, with the extra semantic that it must be the last value selected and initiates form submission
month	A date consisting of a year and a month with no time zone
number	A numerical value
password	Text with no line breaks (sensitive information)
radio	An enumerated value
range	A numerical value, with the extra semantic that the exact value is not important
reset	n/a
search	Text with no line breaks
submit	An enumerated value, with the extra semantic that it must be the last value selected and initiates form submission
tel	Text with no line breaks
text	Text with no line breaks
time	A time (hour, minute, seconds, fractional seconds) with no time zone
url	An absolute IRI
week	A date consisting of a week-year number and a week number with no time zone

Starting the Web Forms Example

In this lesson, we're going to put the new HTML5 controls to work in an example, webforms.html, which you can see in Figure 4.1.

To get started with the webforms.html example, follow these steps:

1. Create webforms.html using a text editor such as Windows WordPad.

2. Enter the following code to create the HTML table that will enclose the web form controls, and add the Submit button.

```
<!DOCTYPE html>
<html>
  <head>
    <title>
      Web Form Example
    </title>
  </head>

  <body>
    <h1>Web Form Example</h1>
    <form method="post" action="webforms.php">
      <table border="1" cellpadding="5">
        .
        .
        .
        <input type="submit" value="Submit">
      </form>
    </body>
</html>
```

3. Save webforms.html. Make sure you save this code in text format (the default format for WordPad, for example, is RTF, rich-text format, which won't work with browsers).

Now that we've started webforms.html, let's begin adding some web form controls.

Creating a Default Control

If you don't specify the type of control you want to create, you'll get a text field, as shown in this task.

Follow these steps:

1. Open webforms.html using a text editor such as Windows WordPad.

2. Add the following code to create a default control, without specifying a type attribute. Note the autofocus attribute, which means that the blinking cursor will appear in this control when the page loads, and the placeholder attribute, which lets you set placeholder text in the control. (This doesn't work in any browser yet.)

```
<!DOCTYPE html>
<html>
  <head>
    <title>
      Web Form Example
    </title>
  </head>

  <body>
    <h1>Web Form Example</h1>
    <form method="post" action="webforms.php">
      <table border="1" cellpadding="5">
      <tr>
      <td>Default</td><td><input name="name"
      placeholder="Enter your nickname" autofocus>
      </td>
      </tr>
        .
        .
        .
      <input type="submit" value="Submit">
    </form>
  </body>
</html>
```

3. Save webforms.html. Make sure you save this code in text format (the default format for WordPad, for example, is RTF, rich-text format, which won't work with browsers).

Now the default control appears as a text field, as you can see at the top of Figure 4.1.

Creating a URL Control

You can also create URL fields; just follow these steps:

1. Open webforms.html using a text editor such as Windows WordPad.

2. Add the following code to create a URL control.

```
<!DOCTYPE html>
<html>
  <head>
    <title>
      Web Form Example
    </title>
  </head>

  <body>
    <h1>Web Form Example</h1>
    <form method="post" action="webforms.php">
      <table border="1" cellpadding="5">
      <tr>
      <td>Default</td><td><input name="name"
      placeholder="Enter your nickname" autofocus>
      </td>
      </tr>
      <tr>
      <td>URL</td><td><input name="url"
        type="url"></td>
      </tr>
        .
        .
        .
      <input type="submit" value="Submit">
    </form>
  </body>
</html>
```

3. Save webforms.html. Make sure you save this code in text format (the default format for WordPad, for example, is RTF, rich-text format, which won't work with browsers).

The browser will try to format the text you entered into this field as a proper URL, starting with http://. If it can't do that, it will display an error.

Creating an Email Control

HTML5 also supports email controls; just follow these steps:

1. Open webforms.html using a text editor such as Windows WordPad.

2. Add the following code.

```
<!DOCTYPE html>
<html>
  <head>
    <title>
      Web Form Example
    </title>
  </head>

  <body>
    <h1>Web Form Example</h1>
    <form method="post" action="webforms.php">
      <table border="1" cellpadding="5">
        .
        .
        .
      <tr>
      <td>Email</td><td><input name="email"
        type="email"></td>
      </tr>
        .
        .
        .
      <input type="submit" value="Submit">
    </form>
  </body>
</html>
```

3. Save webforms.html. Make sure you save this code in text format (the default format for WordPad, for example, is RTF, rich-text format, which won't work with browsers).

The browser will try to format the text you entered into this field as an email address. If it can't, it will display an error, as you see in Figure 4.3.

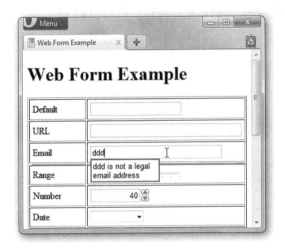

FIGURE 4.3   An email control error.

Creating Range and Number Controls

You can create range and number controls as well; just follow these steps:

1. Open webforms.html using a text editor such as Windows WordPad.

2. Add the following code.

```
<!DOCTYPE html>
<html>
```

```
<head>
 <title>
  Web Form Example
 </title>
</head>

<body>
 <h1>Web Form Example</h1>
 <form method="post" action="webforms.php">
  <table border="1" cellpadding="5">
   .
   .
   .
   <tr>
   <td>Range</td><td><input name="range"
    type="range" min="0" max="100" step="5"
    value="40"></td>
   </tr>
   <td>Number</td><td><input name="number"
    type="number" min="0" max="100"
    step="5" value="40"></td>
   </tr>
   .
   .
   .
   <input type="submit" value="Submit">
  </form>
 </body>
</html>
```

3. Save webforms.html. Make sure you save this code in text format (the default format for WordPad, for example, is RTF, rich-text format, which won't work with browsers).

As you can see in Figure 4.1, the range control displays a slider, and the number control displays up and down arrows. Both allow you to enter a number. Note the min and max attributes, which let you set the allowed range of values, the step attribute, which lets you set the value increment, and the value attribute, which lets you specify the default value of the control.

Creating Date and Time Controls

You can create date and time controls. In this task, we'll create these controls:

► Date

► Time

► Week

► Month

► Datetime

► Local Datetime

To create these controls, follow these steps:

1. Open webforms.html using a text editor such as Windows WordPad.

2. Add the following code.

```
<!DOCTYPE html>
<html>
  <head>
    <title>
       Web Form Example
    </title>
  </head>

  <body>
    <h1>Web Form Example</h1>
    <form method="post" action="webforms.php">
      <table border="1" cellpadding="5">
          .
          .
          .
      <tr>
```

```
<td>Date</td><td><input name="date"
  type="date"></td>
</tr>
<tr>
<td>Week</td><td><input name="week"
  type="week"></td>
</tr>
<tr>
<td>Month</td><td><input name="month"
  type="month"></td>
</tr>
<tr>
<td>Time</td><td><input name="time"
  type="time"></td>
</tr>
<tr>
<td>Datetime</td><td><input name="datetime"
  type="datetime"></td>
</tr>
<tr>
<td>Local Datetime</td><td><input
  name="datetimelocal"
  type="datetime-local"></td>
</tr>
<tr>
  .
  .
  .
  <input type="submit" value="Submit">
</form>
</body>
</html>
```

3. Save webforms.html. Make sure you save this code in text format (the default format for WordPad, for example, is RTF, rich-text format, which won't work with browsers).

To let the user select dates, a date pop-up appears, as shown in Figure 4.4.

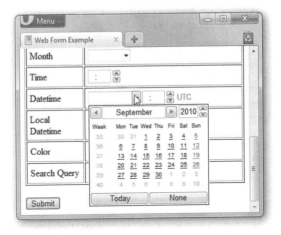

FIGURE 4.4   Date and time controls.

Creating a Color Control

You can let the user select colors with a color control.

Follow these steps:

1. Open webforms.html using a text editor such as Windows WordPad.

2. Add the following code.

```
<!DOCTYPE html>
<html>
  <head>
    <title>
      Web Form Example
    </title>
  </head>

  <body>
    <h1>Web Form Example</h1>
    <form method="post" action="webforms.php">
      <table border="1" cellpadding="5">
          .
          .
          .
```

```
<tr>
<td>Color</td><td><input name="color"
  type="color"></td>
</tr>
   .
   .
   .
   <input type="submit" value="Submit">
  </form>
 </body>
</html>
```

3. Save webforms.html. Make sure you save this code in text format (the default format for WordPad, for example, is RTF, rich-text format, which won't work with browsers).

Currently, you can enter hexadecimal color values (as normally used in HTML) like "ffffff" or "f89f8a" in color controls, but it's not unreasonable to assume that in the future, color pickers that display clickable tables of colors will be used.

Creating a Search Control

You can let the user enter search strings with search controls.

Follow these steps:

1. Open webforms.html using a text editor such as Windows WordPad.

2. Add the following code.

```
<!DOCTYPE html>
<html>
  <head>
    <title>
      Web Form Example
    </title>
  </head>

<body>
  <h1>Web Form Example</h1>
  <form method="post" action="webforms.php">
    <table border="1" cellpadding="5">
       .
```

```
        .
        .
        .
    <tr>
    <td>Search Query</td><td><input name="query"
      type="search"></td>
    </tr>
        .
        .
        .
        <input type="submit" value="Submit">
      </form>
    </body>
  </html>
```

3. Save webforms.html. Make sure you save this code in text format
   (the default format for WordPad, for example, is RTF, rich-text
   format, which won't work with browsers).

The webforms.html Example Code

Following is the full code of the webforms.html example that we developed in this lesson for reference:

```
<!DOCTYPE html>
<html>
  <head>
    <title>
      Web Form Example
    </title>
  </head>

  <body>
    <h1>Web Form Example</h1>
    <form method="post" action="webforms.php">
      <table border="1" cellpadding="5">
      <tr>
      <td>Default</td><td><input name="name"
      placeholder="Enter your nickname" autofocus>
      </td>
      </tr>
      <tr>
      <td>URL</td><td><input name="url"
        type="url"></td>
      </tr>
      <tr>
```

```
<td>Email</td><td><input name="email"
  type="email"></td>
</tr>
<tr>
<tr>
<td>Range</td><td><input name="range"
  type="range" min="0" max="100" step="5"
  value="40"></td>
</tr>
<td>Number</td><td><input name="number"
  type="number" min="0" max="100"
  step="5" value="40"></td>
</tr>
<tr>
<td>Date</td><td><input name="date"
  type="date"></td>
</tr>
<tr>
<td>Week</td><td><input name="week"
  type="week"></td>
</tr>
<tr>
<td>Month</td><td><input name="month"
  type="month"></td>
</tr>
<tr>
<td>Time</td><td><input name="time"
  type="time"></td>
</tr>
<tr>
<td>Datetime</td><td><input name="datetime"
  type="datetime"></td>
</tr>
<tr>
<td>Local Datetime</td><td><input
  name="datetimelocal"
  type="datetime-local"></td>
</tr>
<tr>
<td>Color</td><td><input name="color"
  type="color"></td>
</tr>
<tr>
<td>Search Query</td><td><input name="query"
```

```
      type="search"></td>
    </tr>
    </table>
    <br>
    <input type="submit" value="Submit">
  </form>
 </body>
</html>
```

The webforms.php Example Code

Here's the full code of webforms.php that reads the datetime control and reports its value. If you want to use this code, you'll have to place it on a server that runs PHP in the same directory as webforms.html:

```
<html>
  <head>
    <title>
      Reading data from datetime controls
    </title>
  </head>
  <body>
    <h1>
      Reading data from datetime controls
    </h1>
      You entered:
      <?php
        echo $_REQUEST["datetime"];
      ?>
  </body>
</html>
```

LESSON 5

Inline Editing

HTML5 specifies that you can make elements editable—that is, let the user edit its content. In fact, you can make a whole document editable, which is what we'll discuss in this lesson.

That's not to say that we're talking about text fields either—when you make an element editable, you can include all kinds of elements, such as <div> elements.

In this lesson, we'll make a <div> element editable, which means that when a user clicks it, a text-insertion caret appears, and the user can type. Users can also format the text, as we'll see.

In addition, we'll make a whole document editable, including an <iframe> element. We'll even let users spell check their text.

Let's jump into inline editing now.

Welcome to Inline Editing

You can use three attributes with inline editing:

- ▶ contenteditable—Makes individual HTML elements editable
- ▶ designmode—Makes a whole document editable
- ▶ spellcheck—Enables spellchecking

Let's take a quick look at these attributes.

Making Elements Editable: contenteditable

Works in: Chrome, Firefox, IE, Safari, Opera

In HTML5, you can use the contenteditable attribute to make an element editable. This attribute takes three settings:

- true—Makes the element content editable

- false—Makes the element content not editable

- inherit—Makes this attribute the same as the element's parent element

We'll be setting contenteditable to true in our <div> element in our edit-div.html example to let the user enter text into the <div> element.

Making Documents Editable: designmode

Works in: Chrome, Firefox, IE, Safari, Opera

This attribute is an attribute of the document itself and can make the entire document editable. The designmode attribute can take two settings:

- on—Turns designmode on, which makes the document editable

- off—Turns designmode off, which makes the document not editable

We'll set the document's designmode attribute to "on" in our deditiframe.html example, letting the user edit the document in an <iframe> element.

Enabling Spell Checking: spellcheck

Works in: Firefox

When you edit the content of an element like a <div> element, the browser may let you spellcheck your text. The spellcheck attribute can take two values:

- true—Turn spellchecking on

- false—Turn spellchecking off

We'll see how to use spellchecking in a <div> element in Firefox.

Let's see all this at work in an example, starting by making a <div> element editable in the editdiv.html example.

Starting the editdiv.html Example

In this lesson, we're going to put the new HTML5 contenteditable attribute to work with a <div> element, letting the user enter text as you can see in Figure 5.1.

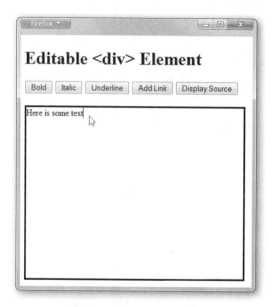

FIGURE 5.1 The editdiv.html example.

We'll also see how to format the text, so this example will include Bold, Italic, and Underline buttons, as you see in the figure. We'll let users add links to their text and see what the final text looks like with the appropriate HTML formatting added when they click the Display Source button.

To get started with the editdiv.html example, follow these steps:

1. Create editdiv.html using a text editor such as Windows WordPad.

2. Enter the following code:

```
<!DOCTYPE html>
<html>
  <head>
    <title>
      Editable &lt;div&gt; Element
    </title>
  </head>

  <body>
    <h1>Editable &lt;div&gt; Element</h1>
        .
        .
        .
  </body>
</html>
```

3. Enter the following code to create the <div> element, setting its contenteditable attribute to true.

```
<!DOCTYPE html>
<html>
  <head>
    <title>
      Editable &lt;div&gt; Element
    </title>
  </head>

  <body>
    <h1>Editable &lt;div&gt; Element</h1>

    <div id="div" style='border:solid
      black; height: 300px; width: 400px'
      contenteditable="true">
    </div>

  </body>
</html>
```

4. Save editdiv.html. Make sure you save this code in text format (the default format for WordPad, for example, is RTF, rich-text format, which won't work with browsers).

Now we've started editdiv.html, as you can see in Figure 5.1.

Adding a Bold Button

You can let the user make text in the editable <div> element bold—and it's easy. Users select the text they want bold with the mouse, and then click the Bold button. It's up to you to then send the command "bold" to the document.

To send the bold command to the document, you use the JavaScript execCommand() function, passing it these argument:

```
object.execCommand(sCommand [, bUserInterface] [, vValue])
```

The arguments mean the following:

▶ sCommand Required—This is a string that specifies the command to execute.

▶ bUserInterface Optional—A true/false value that specifies one of the following:

  ▶ true

    ▶ Display a user interface.

  ▶ false

    ▶ Default. Do not display a user interface.

▶ vValue Optional. Specifies a value to assign.

In this case, we'll send the bold command like this:

```
document.execCommand('bold', false, null);
```

To add the Bold button to this example, follow these steps:

1. Open editdiv.html using a text editor such as Windows WordPad.

2. Add the following code to create a new <div> element for the buttons in this example.

```
<!DOCTYPE html>
<html>
```

```
<head>
  <title>
    Editable &lt;div&gt; Element
  </title>
</head>

<body>
  <h1>Editable &lt;div&gt; Element</h1>
  <div>
        .
        .
        .
  </div>
  <br>
  <div id="div" style='border:solid
    black; height: 300px; width: 400px'
    contenteditable="true">
  </div>

</body>
</html>
```

3. Add the following code to create the Bold button and send the
bold command when it is clicked.

```
<!DOCTYPE html>
<html>
  <head>
    <title>
      Editable &lt;div&gt; Element
    </title>
  </head>

  <body>
    <h1>Editable &lt;div&gt; Element</h1>
    <div>
      <input type="button" value="Bold"
        onclick="document.execCommand('bold', false,
        null);">
    </div>
    <br>
    <div id="div" style='border:solid
      black; height: 300px; width: 400px'
      contenteditable="true">
    </div>
```

```
  </body>
</html>
```

4. Save editdiv.html. Make sure you save this code in text format (the default format for WordPad, for example, is RTF, rich-text format, which won't work with browsers).

Now the user can select text and click the Bold button to make that text bold, as shown in Figure 5.2.

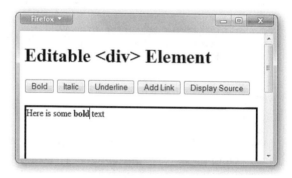

FIGURE 5.2   Bold text in the editdiv.html example.

Adding an Italic Button

You can let the user italicize text with the italic command and an Italic button.

To add that button to the editdiv.html example, follow these steps:

1. Open editdiv.html using a text editor such as Windows WordPad.

2. Add the following code to create the Italic button and send the italic command when it is clicked.

```
<!DOCTYPE html>
<html>
  <head>
    <title>
```

```
    Editable &lt;div&gt; Element
  </title>
</head>

<body>
  <h1>Editable &lt;div&gt; Element</h1>
  <div>
    <input type="button" value="Bold"
      onclick="document.execCommand('bold', false,
      null);">
    <input type="button" value="Italic"
      onclick="document.execCommand
      ('italic', false, null);">
  </div>
  <br>
  <div id="div" style='border:solid
    black; height: 300px; width: 400px'
    contenteditable="true">
  </div>

  </body>
</html>
```

3. Save editdiv.html. Make sure you save this code in text format (the default format for WordPad, for example, is RTF, rich-text format, which won't work with browsers).

Now the user can select text and click the Italic button to make that text italic, as shown in Figure 5.3.

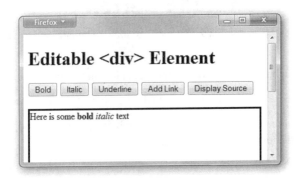

FIGURE 5.3   Italic text in the editdiv.html example.

Adding an Underline Button

You can let the user underline text with the underline command and an Underline button.

To add that button to the editdiv.html example, follow these steps:

1. Open editdiv.html using a text editor such as Windows WordPad.

2. Add the following code to create the Underline button and send the "underline" command when it is clicked.

```
<!DOCTYPE html>
<html>
  <head>
    <title>
      Editable &lt;div&gt; Element
    </title>
  </head>

  <body>
    <h1>Editable &lt;div&gt; Element</h1>
    <div>
      <input type="button" value="Bold"
        onclick="document.execCommand('bold', false,
        null);">
      <input type="button" value="Italic"
        onclick="document.execCommand
        ('italic', false, null);">
      <input type="button" value="Underline"
        onclick="document.execCommand('underline',
        false, null);">
    </div>
    <br>
    <div id="div" style='border:solid
      black; height: 300px; width: 400px'
      contenteditable="true">
    </div>

  </body>
</html>
```

3. Save editdiv.html. Make sure you save this code in text format (the default format for WordPad, for example, is RTF, rich-text format, which won't work with browsers).

Now the user can select text and click the Underline button to make that text underlined, as shown in Figure 5.4.

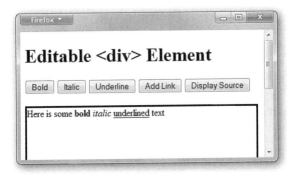

FIGURE 5.4   Underlined text in the editdiv.html example.

Adding an Add Link Button

You can also let the users add links to their text with the createlink command and an Add Link button. When the user selects some text and clicks the Add Link button, we'll pop a dialog box on the screen to let them enter the URL of the link and then create a link of the text they've selected.

To add the Add Link button to the editdiv.html example, follow these steps:

1. Open editdiv.html using a text editor such as Windows WordPad.

2. Add the following code to create the Add Link button and call the createlink() function.

```
<!DOCTYPE html>
<html>
  <head>
    <title>
      Editable &lt;div&gt; Element
    </title>

  </head>

  <body>
```

```
<h1>Editable &lt;div&gt; Element</h1>
<div>
  <input type="button" value="Bold"
    onclick="document.execCommand('bold', false,
    null);">
  <input type="button" value="Italic"
    onclick="document.execCommand
    ('italic', false, null);">
  <input type="button" value="Underline"
    onclick="document.execCommand('underline',
    false, null);">
  <input type="button" value="Add Link"
    onclick="createLink();">
</div>
<br>
<div id="div" style='border:solid
  black; height: 300px; width: 400px'
  contenteditable="true">
</div>

</body>
</html>
```

3. Add the following JavaScript code to get the URL of the link
from the user with a dialog box and then add that URL to the
link with the createlink command:

```
<!DOCTYPE html>
<html>
  <head>
    <title>
      Editable &lt;div&gt; Element
    </title>

    <script type="text/javascript">
      function createLink()
      {
        var url = prompt("Enter URL:", "http://");
        if (url)
          document.execCommand("createlink",
            false, url);
      }
    </script>
  </head>

  <body>
```

```
<h1>Editable &lt;div&gt; Element</h1>
<div>
  <input type="button" value="Bold"
    onclick="document.execCommand('bold', false,
    null);">
  <input type="button" value="Italic"
    onclick="document.execCommand
    ('italic', false, null);">
  <input type="button" value="Underline"
    onclick="document.execCommand('underline',
    false, null);">
  <input type="button" value="Add Link"
    onclick="createLink();">
</div>
<br>
<div id="div" style='border:solid
  black; height: 300px; width: 400px'
  contenteditable="true">
</div>

  </body>
</html>
```

4. Save editdiv.html. Make sure you save this code in text format
   (the default format for WordPad, for example, is RTF, rich-text
   format, which won't work with browsers).

Now the user can select text and click the Add Link button to make that
text into a hyperlink, as shown in Figure 5.5 (the link was underlined with
the Underline button).

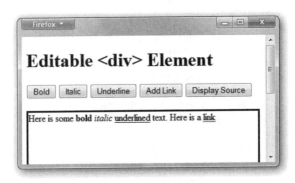

FIGURE 5.5   A link in the editdiv.html example.

Adding a Display Source Button

When users are done formatting their text, you can let them display the HTML of that text when they click a Display Source button. For example, the HTML for the text shown in Figure 5.5 is

```
Here is some <span style="font-weight: bold;">bold </span><span
style="font-style: italic;">italic </span><span style="text-
decoration: underline;">underlined </span>text! Here is a <a
href="http://www.usatoday.com"><span style="text-decoration:
underline;">link</span></a>.
```

To add the Display Source button to the editdiv.html example, follow these steps:

1. Open editdiv.html using a text editor such as Windows WordPad.

2. Add the following code to create the Display Source button and call the showSource() function.

```
<!DOCTYPE html>
<html>
  <head>
    <title>
      Editable &lt;div&gt; Element
    </title>

  </head>

  <body>
    <h1>Editable &lt;div&gt; Element</h1>
    <div>
      <input type="button" value="Bold"
        onclick="document.execCommand('bold', false,
        null);">
      <input type="button" value="Italic"
        onclick="document.execCommand
        ('italic', false, null);">
      <input type="button" value="Underline"
        onclick="document.execCommand('underline',
        false, null);">
      <input type="button" value="Add Link"
        onclick="createLink();">
      <input type="button"
      value="Display Source"
      onclick="showSource();">
    </div>
```

```
<br>
<div id="div" style='border:solid
   black; height: 300px; width: 400px'
   contenteditable="true">
</div>

</body>
</html>
```

3. Add the following JavaScript code to read the HTML source
from the innerHTML property of the <div> element and display
that source in a dialog box:

```
<!DOCTYPE html>
<html>
  <head>
    <title>
       Editable &lt;div&gt; Element
    </title>

    <script type="text/javascript">
      function showSource()
      {
        var content = document.getElementById
          ("div").innerHTML;
        content.replace(/</g,'&lt;');
        content.replace(/>/g, '&gt;');
        alert(content);
      }

      function createLink()
      {
        var url = prompt("Enter URL:", "http://");
        if (url)
          document.execCommand("createlink",
            false, url);
      }
    </script>
  </head>

  <body>
    <h1>Editable &lt;div&gt; Element</h1>
    <div>
      <input type="button" value="Bold"
        onclick="document.execCommand('bold', false,
```

```
      null);">
    <input type="button" value="Italic"
      onclick="document.execCommand
      ('italic', false, null);">
    <input type="button" value="Underline"
      onclick="document.execCommand('underline',
      false, null);">
    <input type="button" value="Add Link"
      onclick="createLink();">
  </div>
  <br>
  <div id="div" style='border:solid
    black; height: 300px; width: 400px'
    contenteditable="true">
  </div>

  </body>
</html>
```

4. Save editdiv.html. Make sure you save this code in text format
(the default format for WordPad, for example, is RTF, rich-text
format, which won't work with browsers).

Now the user can click the Display Source button to see the HTML source
of the text in the <div> element, as shown in Figure 5.6.

FIGURE 5.6   Displaying the HTML source in the editdiv.html example.

Spellchecking

If your browser supports it—and that's only Firefox now—you can
spellcheck the text you enter in editable elements and documents.
Spellchecking is on by default in Firefox.

> TIP: To turn spellchecking off in Firefox, set the spellcheck attribute of the editable element or document to false.

To spellcheck your text in Firefox, follow these steps:

1. Enter your text in an editable element or document. Firefox will underline words it considers misspelled with a wavy red underline, as you see in Figure 5.7.

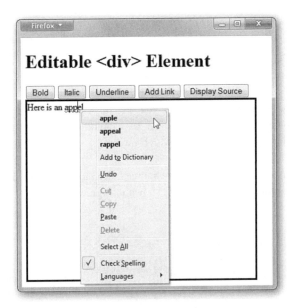

FIGURE 5.7   Spellchecking in Firefox.

2. Right-click a word that Firefox has identified as misspelled. This pops up a menu of possible correct spellings, as you can see in Figure 5.7.

3. Select a correct spelling from the pop-up menu. Firefox inserts the correct spelling into your text.

The editdiv.html Example Code

Here is the whole editdiv.html example code:

```html
<!DOCTYPE html>
<html>
  <head>
    <title>
      Editable &lt;div&gt; Element
    </title>

    <script type="text/javascript">
      function showSource()
      {
        var content = document.getElementById
          ("div").innerHTML;
        content.replace(/</g,'&lt;');
        content.replace(/>/g, '&gt;');
        alert(content);
      }

      function createLink()
      {
        var url = prompt("Enter URL:", "http://");
        if (url)
          document.execCommand("createlink",
            false, url);
      }
    </script>
  </head>

  <body>
    <h1>Editable &lt;div&gt; Element</h1>
    <div>
      <input type="button" value="Bold"
        onclick="document.execCommand('bold', false,
        null);">
      <input type="button" value="Italic"
        onclick="document.execCommand
        ('italic', false, null);">
      <input type="button" value="Underline"
        onclick="document.execCommand('underline',
        false, null);">
      <input type="button" value="Add Link"
        onclick="createLink();">
```

```
   <input type="button"
    value="Display Source"
    onclick="showSource();">
 </div>
 <br>
 <div id="div" style='border:solid
   black; height: 300px; width: 400px'
   contenteditable="true">
 </div>

</body>
</html>
```

Starting the editiframe.html Example

Now we're going to put the new HTML5 designmode attribute, which makes a whole document editable, to work with an <iframe> floating frame, letting the user enter text, as you can see in Figure 5.8. Here, using the designmode attribute of the <iframe> will make the entire <iframe>— and any elements you might want to add to it—editable. So instead of just making a <div> editable, now a whole document, contained in an <iframe> will be editable.

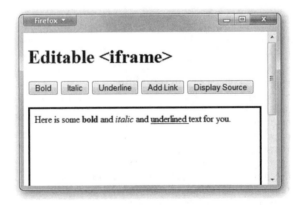

FIGURE 5.8   The editiframe.html example.

As in the editdiv.html example, the user can click buttons to format the text.

To get started with the editiframe.html example, follow these steps:

1. Create editframe.html using a text editor such as Windows WordPad.

2. Enter the following code, creating this example and the <iframe>.

```
<!DOCTYPE html>
<html>
  <head>
    <title>
      Editable &lt;iframe&gt;
    </title>

  </head>

  <body onload="loader()">
    <h1>Editable &lt;iframe&gt;</h1>
    <iframe id="content" style='border:solid
      black; height: 300px; width: 400px'
      src="about:blank">
    </iframe>
  </body>
</html>
```

3. Enter the following code to set the designmode attribute of the <iframe> to on.

```
<!DOCTYPE html>
<html>
  <head>
    <title>
      Editable &lt;iframe&gt;
    </title>

    <script type="text/javascript">
    var iframe;

    function loader()
    {
      iframe =
        document.getElementById("content");
      iframe.contentDocument.designMode = "on";
    }
      .

      .
```

```
       window.addEventListener("loader", onload,
          false);
       </script>
    </head>

    <body onload="loader()">
       <h1>Editable &lt;iframe&gt;</h1>
       <iframe id="content" style='border:solid
          black; height: 300px; width: 400px'
          src="about:blank">
       </iframe>
    </body>
</html>
```

4. Save editiframe.html. Make sure you save this code in text format (the default format for WordPad, for example, is RTF, rich-
text format, which won't work with browsers).

We've started editiframe.html, created the <iframe>, and set its designmode attribute to on. Next, we'll add the formatting buttons.

Adding the editiframe.html Buttons

Now we can add the buttons to the editiframe.html example. Because
those buttons work the same way as in the editdiv.html example, we won't
spend a lot of time here.

To add the buttons to the editiframe.html example, follow these steps:

1. Open editframe.html using a text editor such as Windows
WordPad.

2. Add the following code, adding the buttons to this example.

```
<!DOCTYPE html>
<html>
   <head>
      <title>
         Editable &lt;iframe&gt;
      </title>
```

```
<script type="text/javascript">
var iframe;

function loader()
{
  iframe =
    document.getElementById("content");
  iframe.contentDocument.designMode = "on";
}

function showSource()
{
  var content =
    iframe.contentDocument.body.innerHTML;
  content.replace(/</g, '&lt;');
  content.replace(/>/g, '&gt;');
  alert(content);
}

function createLink()
{
    var url = prompt("Enter URL:", "http://");
    if (url)
      iframe.contentDocument.execCommand
        ("createlink", false, url);
}

window.addEventListener("loader", onload,
  false);
</script>
</head>

<body onload="loader()">
  <h1>Editable &lt;iframe&gt;</h1>
  <div>
    <input type="button" value="Bold" onclick=
      "iframe.contentDocument.execCommand
      ('bold', false, null);">
    <input type="button" value="Italic"
      onclick="iframe.contentDocument.execCommand
      ('italic', false, null);">
    <input type="button" value="Underline"
      onclick="iframe.contentDocument.execCommand
      ('underline', false, null);">
    <input type="button" value="Add Link"
```

```
      onclick="createLink();">
    <input type="button" value="Display Source"
      onclick="showSource();">
  </div>
  <br>
  <iframe id="content" style='border:solid
    black; height: 300px; width: 400px'
    src="about:blank">
  </iframe>
  </body>
</html>
```

3. Save editiframe.html. Make sure you save this code in text format (the default format for WordPad, for example, is RTF, rich-text format, which won't work with browsers).

That completes the editiframe.html example, which you can see at work in Figure 5.8. To all appearances, this example functions the same way as the editdiv.html example, except that here the user is editing the entire document in an <iframe>.

The editiframe.html Example Code

Here is the whole editiframe.html example code:

```
<!DOCTYPE html>
<html>
  <head>
    <title>
      Editable &lt;iframe&gt;
    </title>

    <script type="text/javascript">
    var iframe;

    function loader()
    {
      iframe =
        document.getElementById("content");
      iframe.contentDocument.designMode = "on";
    }

    function showSource()
```

```
  {
    var content =
      iframe.contentDocument.body.innerHTML;
    content.replace(/</g, '&lt;');
    content.replace(/>/g, '&gt;');
    alert(content);
  }

  function createLink()
  {
    var url = prompt("Enter URL:", "http://");
    if (url)
      iframe.contentDocument.execCommand
        ("createlink", false, url);
  }

  window.addEventListener("loader", onload,
    false);
  </script>
</head>

<body onload="loader()">
  <h1>Editable &lt;iframe&gt;</h1>
  <div>
    <input type="button" value="Bold" onclick=
      "iframe.contentDocument.execCommand
      ('bold', false, null);">
    <input type="button" value="Italic"
      onclick="iframe.contentDocument.execCommand
      ('italic', false, null);">
    <input type="button" value="Underline"
      onclick="iframe.contentDocument.execCommand
      ('underline', false, null);">
    <input type="button" value="Add Link"
      onclick="createLink();">
    <input type="button" value="Display Source"
      onclick="showSource();">
  </div>
  <br>
  <iframe id="content" style='border:solid
    black; height: 300px; width: 400px'
    src="about:blank">
  </iframe>
</body>
</html>
```

LESSON 6

Working with Browser History

HTML5 gives you control over the browser's history—where it's been and where it is now. The History object lets you move forward and backward, from page to page in the browser, which means you can use the history object, for example, to go back three pages.

You can also store data in a browser's history state object. That is, you can add data to the state object and then *push* that state object to store it with the current page. You can also pop the state object, recovering the data you stored, which allows you to pass data from page to page.

We'll see how all this works in the current lesson. Let's jump into browser history now.

Welcome to Browser History

In this lesson, we'll develop an example named pophistory.html, which you can see in Figure 6.1.

This example illustrates the different aspects of the HTML history object. The user can click the Back button to go back one page (just like clicking the browser's Back button). The user can click the Forward button to go forward one page (if there is no next page, nothing happens).

You can also enter an integer in the text field and click the Go button to move, for example, five pages ahead. Entering a negative number takes you into the pages the browser has already been to.

In addition, the example displays the length of the browser history, as you can see in Figure 6.1; making that length accessible is part of the HTML5 specification.

FIGURE 6.1   The pophistory.html example.

Finally, the example lets the user enter some text and push that text as data in the current history state, then go to another page and come back—and when the state object is popped, the text you entered is displayed. In this way, you can pass data from page to page.

To make the pushing and popping of data work, you need a browser that supports this part of the history functionality. Unfortunately, there are no official releases of any browsers that support this yet. Nonetheless, we'll see how this works in code so you'll be ready when the browsers are.

Next, let's see some of the details behind this example.

Getting to Know the History API

The history object is part of the window object in the browser, so you can refer to it as the window.history object. Following are the attributes and functions you use to implement window.history support in HTML5:

- ▶ window.history.length;
- ▶ window.history.go();
- ▶ window.history.back();
- ▶ window.history.forward();

- window.history.pushState();

- window.history.replaceState();

- window.onpopstate

We'll take a closer look at them now.

window.history.length

The window.history.length attribute gives the number of entries in the browser session history. We'll take a look at this attribute in the pophistory.html example.

window.history.back()

This function goes back one step in the browser history. That is, it returns the browser to the previous page.

If there was no previous page, this function does nothing.

window.history.forward()

This function moves forward one step in the browser history. That is, if you went to another page, page A, then returned to the current page and executed this function, you'd return to page A.

Note that if there is no next page in the browser history, this function does nothing.

window.history.go([*delta*])

This is a general purpose function that lets you move forward or backward by the number of pages you specify with *delta*. For example, passing a value of -2 makes the browser go back two pages; passing a value of 5 makes the browser go ahead five pages.

The *delta* argument is in brackets because it's optional. If you don't supply a *delta*, however, the browser just reloads the current page.

And, as you'd expect, if *delta* is out of history range, this function does nothing.

window.history.pushState(*data, title* [, *url*])

This function lets you push data into the history. The *data* argument is an object that contains your data, *title* is the name with which you want to reference that data, and the *url* argument lets you associate the data with a particular page so it'll be popped when that page is reloaded.

window.history.replaceState(*data, title* [, *url*])

This function replaces the current entry in the history to have the given data, title, and, if you give it, URL.

window.onpopstate

This event occurs when the state history is popped and so becomes accessible—including the data you pushed. We'll see how to put this event to work in pophistory.html.

Starting the pophistory.html Example

To get started with the pophistory.html example, follow these steps:

1. Create pophistory.html using a text editor such as Windows WordPad.

2. Enter the following code.

```
<!DOCTYPE html>
<html>
  <head>
    <title>
      Page to Page History
    </title>

  </head>

  <body>
    <h1>Page to Page History</h1>
```

```
      .
      .
      .
   </body>
</html>
```

3. Add the following code to create the <div> elements this example uses to display results.

```
<!DOCTYPE html>
<html>
  <head>
    <title>
      Page to Page History
    </title>

  </head>

  <body onload="loader()">
    <h1>Page to Page History</h1>
    <br>
    <div id="length"></div>
    <br>
    <div id="state"></div>
    <br>
  </body>
</html>
```

4. Save pophistory.html. Make sure you save this code in text format (the default format for WordPad, for example, is RTF, rich-
text format, which won't work with browsers).

We've started pophistory.html. Now let's make it do something.

Adding a Back Button

You can let the user navigate backward in the browser history with the
window.history.back() function. To add the Back button to this example,
follow these steps:

1. Open pophistory.html using a text editor such as Windows
WordPad.

2. Add the following code to create a new Back button.

```
<!DOCTYPE html>
<html>
  <head>
    <title>
      Page to Page History
    </title>

  </head>

  <body onload="loader()">
    <h1>Page to Page History</h1>
    <input type="button" value="Back"
      onclick="back();">
          .
          .
          .

    <br>
    <div id="length"></div>
    <br>
    <div id="state"></div>
    <br>
  </body>
</html>
```

3. Add the following code to make the Back button active by con-
    necting it to the window.history.back() function.

```
<!DOCTYPE html>
<html>
  <head>
    <title>
      Page to Page History
    </title>

    <script type="text/javascript">
      function back()
      {
        window.history.back();
      }
    </script>
  </head>

  <body onload="loader()">
    <h1>Page to Page History</h1>
    <input type="button" value="Back"
      onclick="back();">
    <br>
```

```
    <div id="length"></div>
    <br>
    <div id="state"></div>
    <br>
  </body>
</html>
```

4. Save pophistory.html. Make sure you save this code in text format (the default format for WordPad, for example, is RTF, rich-text format, which won't work with browsers).

Now the user can click the Back button, which appears in Figure 6.1, to navigate the browser back one page. For example, you might go to www. usatoday.com, as shown in Figure 6.2, then to the pophistory.html page, as shown in Figure 6.3, and click the Back button, which would take you back to www.usatoday.com, as shown in Figure 6.4.

FIGURE 6.2   The *USA Today* page.

FIGURE 6.3   Navigating to the pophistory.html page.

FIGURE 6.4   Back to *USA Today.*

Adding a Forward Button

You can also let the user navigate forward in the browser history with the window.history.forward() function. To add the Forward button to this example, follow these steps:

1. Open pophistory.html using a text editor such as Windows WordPad.

2. Add the following code to create a new Forward button.

```
<!DOCTYPE html>
<html>
  <head>
    <title>
      Page to Page History
    </title>

  </head>

  <body onload="loader()">
    <h1>Page to Page History</h1>
    <input type="button" value="Back"
      onclick="back();">
    <input type="button" value="Forward"
      onclick="forward();">
    <br>

          .
          .
          .

    <br>
    <div id="length"></div>
    <br>
    <div id="state"></div>
    <br>
  </body>
</html>
```

3. Add the following code to make the Forward button active by connecting it to the window.history.forward() function.

```
<!DOCTYPE html>
<html>
  <head>
    <title>
      Page to Page History
    </title>

    <script type="text/javascript">
      function back()
      {
        window.history.back();
      }

      function forward()
      {
        window.history.forward();
      }
    </script>
  </head>
```

```
<body onload="loader()">
  <h1>Page to Page History</h1>
  <input type="button" value="Back"
    onclick="back();">
  <br>
  <input type="button" value="Forward"
    onclick="forward();">
  <br>
  <div id="length"></div>
  <br>
  <div id="state"></div>
  <br>
</body>
</html>
```

4. Save pophistory.html. Make sure you save this code in text format (the default format for WordPad, for example, is RTF, rich-
   text format, which won't work with browsers).

When the user clicks the Forward button, the browser navigates forward
one page in the browser history.

Adding a Go Button

You can let users specify how many pages forward or backward they want
to navigate the browser by entering an integer (positive means forward,
negative means backward) into a text field and clicking a Go button, which
will use the window.history.go() function to navigate the browser.

To add the Go button to this example, follow these steps:

1. Open pophistory.html using a text editor such as Windows
   WordPad.

2. Add the following code to create a new text field and a Go button.

```
<!DOCTYPE html>
<html>
  <head>
    <title>
      Page to Page History
    </title>

  </head>
```

```
<body onload="loader()">
  <h1>Page to Page History</h1>
  <input type="button" value="Back"
    onclick="back();">
  <input type="button" value="Forward"
    onclick="forward();">
  <br>
  Pages to move by: <input id="amount"
    type="text">
  <input type="button" value="Go" onclick="go();">
  <br>
      .
      .
      .

  <br>
  <div id="length"></div>
  <br>
  <div id="state"></div>
  <br>
</body>
</html>
```

3. Add the following code to make the Go button active by connecting it to the window.history.go() function.

```
<!DOCTYPE html>
<html>
  <head>
    <title>
      Page to Page History
    </title>

    <script type="text/javascript">
      function back()
      {
        window.history.back();
      }

      function forward()
      {
        window.history.forward();
      }
```

```
function go()
{
  var amount =
    document.getElementById
    ("amount").value;
    window.history.go(amount);
}
</script>
</head>

<body onload="loader()">
  <h1>Page to Page History</h1>
  <input type="button" value="Back"
    onclick="back();">
  <br>
  <input type="button" value="Forward"
    onclick="forward();">
  <br>
  <div id="length"></div>
  <br>
  <div id="state"></div>
  <br>
  Pages to move by: <input id="amount"
    type="text">
  <input type="button" value="Go" onclick="go();">
  <br>
</body>
</html>
```

4. Save pophistory.html. Make sure you save this code in text for-
    mat (the default format for WordPad, for example, is RTF, rich-
    text format, which won't work with browsers).

When the user enters a number in the text field and clicks the Go button,
the browser navigates forward or backward a matching number of pages.

Getting History Length

You can determine the total number of pages in the browser's history (both
forward and backward entries) with the window.history.length attribute.
We'll display that length in pophistory.html; to do so, follow these steps:

1. Open pophistory.html using a text editor such as Windows WordPad.

2. Add the following code to display the number of entries in the
    history in a <div> element in pophistory.html.

```html
<!DOCTYPE html>
<html>
  <head>
    <title>
      Page to Page History
    </title>

    <script type="text/javascript">
      function back()
      {
        window.history.back();
      }

      function forward()
      {
        window.history.forward();
      }

      function loader()
      {
        var length = window.history.length;
        document.getElementById
          ("length").innerHTML = "<h1>" +
          "History length: " + length +
          "</h1>";
      }

    </script>
  </head>

  <body onload="loader()">
    <h1>Page to Page History</h1>
    <input type="button" value="Back"
      onclick="back();">
    <br>
    <input type="button" value="Forward"
      onclick="forward();">
    <br>
    <div id="length"></div>
    <br>
    <div id="state"></div>
    <br>
    Pages to move by: <input id="amount"
      type="text">
    <input type="button" value="Go" onclick="go();">
    <br>
  </body>
</html>
```

3. Save pophistory.html. Make sure you save this code in text format (the default format for WordPad, for example, is RTF, rich-text format, which won't work with browsers).

Now when the page loads, it'll display the number of entries in the window history, as shown in Figure 6.5.

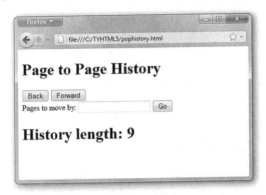

FIGURE 6.5   Window history length.

Pushing Data into the History

You can let the user push text data into the current page's history, to be recovered later. Here's how:

1. Open pophistory.html using a text editor such as Windows WordPad.

2. Add the following code to display a text field and a button with the caption Push Data.

```
<!DOCTYPE html>
<html>
  <head>
    <title>
      Page to Page History
    </title>

      function forward()
      {
        window.history.forward();
      }

    </script>
  </head>
```

```
<body onload="loader()">
  <h1>Page to Page History</h1>
  <input type="button" value="Back"
    onclick="back();">
  <br>
  <input type="button" value="Forward"
    onclick="forward();">
  <br>
  <br>
  <br>
  Text to push: <input id="statedata"
    type="text">
  <input type="button" value="Push Data"
    onclick="pushdata();">
  <br>
  <div id="length"></div>
  <br>
  <div id="state"></div>
  <br>
  Pages to move by: <input id="amount"
    type="text">
  <input type="button" value="Go" onclick="go();">
  <br>
</body>
</html>
```

3. Add the following code to add the text the user entered to an object, then push that object into the current page's history (so it will be popped when you return to this page).

```
<!DOCTYPE html>
<html>
  <head>
    <title>
      Page to Page History
    </title>

    <script type="text/javascript">
      function back()
      {
        window.history.back();
      }

      function forward()
      {
        window.history.forward();
      }
```

```
function pushData()
{
  var statedata =
  document.getElementById
  ("statedata").value;
  var containerObject =
  {container: statedata};
  history.pushState(containerObject,
  "item", "pophistory.html");
}

</script>
</head>

<body onload="loader()">
  <h1>Page to Page History</h1>
  <input type="button" value="Back"
    onclick="back();">
  <br>
  <input type="button" value="Forward"
    onclick="forward();">
  <br>
  <br>
  <br>
  Text to push: <input id="statedata"
    type="text">
  <input type="button" value="Push Data"
    onclick="pushdata();">
  <br>
  <div id="length"></div>
  <br>
  <div id="state"></div>
  <br>
  Pages to move by: <input id="amount"
    type="text">
  <input type="button" value="Go" onclick="go();">
  <br>
  </body>
</html>
```

4. Save pophistory.html. Make sure you save this code in text format (the default format for WordPad, for example, is RTF, rich-text format, which won't work with browsers).

Now when the user enters data in the text field and clicks the Push Data button, that text will be pushed into the history of the current page. In the next task, we'll see about recovering that pushed text.

Popping Data from the History

Because we've pushed data into the current page's history state, it'll be popped automatically when the current page is reloaded, and we can recover the data the user pushed. Here's how to do that and display that data by connecting a function to the onpopstate event for the page:

1. Open pophistory.html using a text editor such as Windows WordPad.

2. Add the following code to the onpopstate event, which will recover the text the user pushed and display it in a <div> element.

```
<!DOCTYPE html>
<html>
  <head>
    <title>
      Page to Page History
    </title>

    <script type="text/javascript">
      function go()
      {
        var amount =
          document.getElementById
          ("amount").value;
        window.history.go(amount);
      }

      function back()
      {
        window.history.back();
      }

      function forward()
      {
        window.history.forward();
      }

      function pushData()
```

```
      {
        var statedata =
          document.getElementById
          ("statedata").value;
        var containerObject =
          {container: statedata};
        history.pushState(containerObject,
          "item", "pophistory.html");
      }

      function popData(event)
      {
        var state = "Page: " +
          document.location + " Data: " +
          event.state.container;
        document.getElementById
          ("state").innerHTML = "<h1>" +
          state + "</h1>";
      };

      window.addEventListener("popstate", popData,
        false);
    </script>
  </head>

  <body onload="loader()">
    <h1>Page to Page History</h1>
    <input type="button" value="Back"
      onclick="back();">
    <input type="button" value="Forward"
      onclick="forward();">
    <br>
    Pages to move by: <input id="amount"
      type="text">
    <input type="button" value="Go" onclick="go();">
    <br>
    <br>
    <br>
    Text to push: <input id="statedata"
      type="text">
    <input type="button" value="Push Data"
      onclick="pushdata();">
    <br>
    <div id="length"></div>
    <br>
```

```
    <div id="state"></div>
    <br>
  </body>
</html>
```

3. Save pophistory.html. Make sure you save this code in text format (the default format for WordPad, for example, is RTF, rich-text format, which won't work with browsers).

Now when the user enters text into the pophistory.html page, clicks the Push Data page, navigates to a new page, then returns to the pophistory.html page, the text will be popped and displayed automatically.

As mentioned, this functionality isn't supported by any officially released browser yet, but now you're ready when support for this feature appears.

The pophistory.html Example Code

Here is the whole pophistory.html example code:

```
<!DOCTYPE html>
<html>
  <head>
    <title>
      Page to Page History
    </title>

    <script type="text/javascript">
      function go()
      {
        var amount =
          document.getElementById
          ("amount").value;
        window.history.go(amount);
      }

      function back()
      {
        window.history.back();
      }

      function forward()
```

```
    {
      window.history.forward();
    }

    function loader()
    {
      var length = window.history.length;
      document.getElementById
        ("length").innerHTML = "<h1>" +
        "History length: " + length +
        "</h1>";
    }

    function pushData()
    {
      var statedata =
        document.getElementById
        ("statedata").value;
      var containerObject =
        {container: statedata};
      history.pushState(containerObject,
        "item", "pophistory.html");
    }

    function popData(event)
    {
      var state = "Page: " +
        document.location + " Data: " +
        event.state.container;
      document.getElementById
          ("state").innerHTML = "<h1>" +
          state + "</h1>";
    };

    window.addEventListener("popstate", popData,
      false);
  </script>
</head>

<body onload="loader()">
  <h1>Page to Page History</h1>
  <input type="button" value="Back"
    onclick="back();">
  <input type="button" value="Forward"
    onclick="forward();">
```

```
    <br>
    Pages to move by: <input id="amount"
      type="text">
    <input type="button" value="Go" onclick="go();">
    <br>
    <br>
    <br>
    Text to push: <input id="statedata"
      type="text">
    <input type="button" value="Push Data"
      onclick="pushdata();">
    <br>
    <div id="length"></div>
    <br>
    <div id="state"></div>
    <br>
  </body>
</html>
```

LESSON 7

Getting the Point Across with Messaging

HTML5 lets you send messages in a cross-window or cross-domain way; we'll see how that works in this lesson.

Say, for example, that in page A, page B—which comes from the same directory on the server—appears in an <iframe> element. Now you can send text messages from page A to page B and make use of those messages in page B. That's cross-window messaging.

In fact, page B can come from an entirely different domain and still appear in the <iframe> in page A, and you can still send messages to page A. That's called cross-domain messaging, and it used to be prohibited, but now you can do it. So even if page B comes from an entirely different server than page A, you can still send page B messages.

We'll see how all this works in the current lesson. Let's jump into messaging now.

Welcome to Messaging

In this lesson, we'll develop an example named parent.html, which you can see in Figure 7.1.

That's an <iframe> element you see outlined in black in Figure 7.1. It contains a second page, child.html, from the same directory as parent.html itself. So now you can send messages between windows in the same application.

You can enter a message in the text field in this example, as you see in Figure 7.1, and when you click the button, that message is sent to and

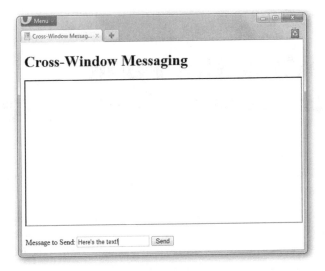

FIGURE 7.1   The parent.html and child.html example.

echoed by the second page in the <iframe>, as shown in Figure 7.2. This is a good example of cross-window messaging.

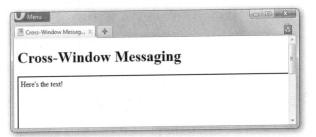

FIGURE 7.2   Sending a cross-window message.

The second example in this lesson will show how to use cross-domain messaging, where the windows are in different Internet domains. This time, the domainparent.html page shown in Figure 7.3 is from a different domain than the page, domainchild.html, that appears in the <iframe> element, as shown in Figure 7.3.

You can enter a message in the text field as shown in Figure 7.3 and click the button to send that message cross-domain from domainparent.html to

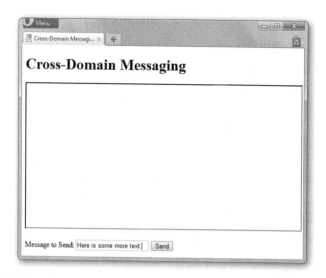

FIGURE 7.3 The domainparent.html and domainchild.html example.

domainchild.html. The domainchild.html page echoes the message, as you can see in Figure 7.4.

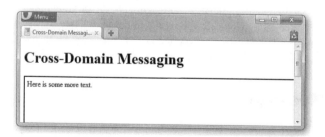

FIGURE 7.4 Sending a cross-domain message.

Let's see some of the details behind this example now.

Getting to Know the Messaging API

You make messaging work behind the scenes with a scripting language like JavaScript. You can find a good introduction to messaging at

www.whatwg.org/specs/web-apps/current-work/multipage/comms.html

Here are the scripting features you use with messaging:

- ▶ postMessage() function
- ▶ onMessage event
- ▶ event.data attribute
- ▶ event.origin attribute
- ▶ event.source attribute

We'll take a closer look at these items now.

postMessage()

Supported browsers: Opera, Safari

This function is the core of sending messages in HTML5, and you use it to post a message to a target:

```
window . postMessage(message, targetOrigin)
```

Here, message is the text message you are posting to the *target*, and *targetOrigin* is the *origin* of the target. We'll see more about origins when it becomes time to send messages in this lesson; the origin uniquely specifies the target (as by URL). If you send a message to a target that doesn't match the origin you pass to postMessage(), the message is discarded. To match any origin, you can pass a value of "*:

onMessage

Supported browsers: Opera, Safari

This is the event that occurs when a message is received. You connect a function to this message, and then you can recover the actual message sent by examining the event object's data member.

event.data

Supported browsers: Opera, Safari

The event object passed to the onMessage handler contains the information about the message you need—the data attribute contains the message's text.

event.origin

Supported browsers: Opera, Safari

The event.origin attribute contains the origin that the message was sent to.

event.source

Supported browsers: Opera, Safari

The event.source attribute contains the WindowProxy of the source window.

Let's put all this to work with an example, starting with the cross-window parent.html/child.html example.

Starting the parent.html Example

To get started with the parent.html example, follow these steps:

1. Create parent.html using a text editor such as Windows WordPad.

2. Enter the following code.

```
<!DOCTYPE html>

<html>
  <head>
    <title>
      Cross-Window Messaging
    </title>

  </head>

  <body>
    <h1>Cross-Window Messaging</h1>
  </body>
```

3. Add the following code to create the <iframe> element this example uses to display child.html in, as well as a text field to

accept the message to send, and a button connected to a function
named send() to send the message.

```html
<!DOCTYPE html>

<html>
  <head>
    <title>
      Cross-Window Messaging
    </title>

  </head>

  <body>
    <h1>Cross-Window Messaging</h1>
    <iframe id="iframe" src="child.html"
      height="300" width="600">
    </iframe>
    <br>
    <br>
    Message to Send: <input id="message"
      type="text">
    <input type="button" onclick="send();"
      value="Send">
  </body>
```

4. Save parent.html. Make sure you save this code in text format
   (the default format for WordPad, for example, is RTF, rich-text
   format, which won't work with browsers).

We've started parent.html. Now let's make it send the message.

Sending a Cross-Window Message

You can send a message from parent.html to child.html by following these
steps:

1. Open parent.html using a text editor such as Windows WordPad.

2. Add the following code to implement the send() function that
   sends the message, which starts by getting the message and some
   information about the target window.

```
<!DOCTYPE html>

<html>
  <head>
    <title>
      Cross-Window Messaging
    </title>

    <script type="text/javascript">
    function send()
    {
      var message =
        document.getElementById("message").value;
      var location = window.location;
      var protocol = location.protocol;
      var host = location.host;
      .
      .
      .
    }
    </script>
  </head>

  <body>
    <h1>Cross-Window Messaging</h1>
    <iframe id="iframe" src="child.html"
      height="300" width="600">
    </iframe>
    <br>
    <br>
    Message to Send: <input id="message"
      type="text">
    <input type="button" onclick="send();"
      value="Send">
  </body>
```

3. Add the following code to send the message to the target window.

```
<!DOCTYPE html>

<html>
  <head>
    <title>
      Cross-Window Messaging
    </title>

    <script type="text/javascript">
```

```
function send()
{
  var message =
    document.getElementById("message").value;
  var location = window.location;
  var protocol = location.protocol;
  var host = location.host;
  document.getElementById
    ("iframe").contentWindow.postMessage
      (message, protocol + "//" + host);
}
</script>
</head>

<body>
  <h1>Cross-Window Messaging</h1>
  <iframe id="iframe" src="child.html"
    height="300" width="600">
  </iframe>
  <br>
  <br>
  Message to Send: <input id="message"
    type="text">
  <input type="button" onclick="send();"
    value="Send">
</body>
```

4. Save parent.html. Make sure you save this code in text format (the default format for WordPad, for example, is RTF, rich-text format, which won't work with browsers).

Now the user can enter a message into the text field, as shown in Figure 7.1, and click the button to send the message to child.html. Let's build child.html next (don't try to run parent.html until you've created child.html).

Starting the child.html Example

To get started with the child.html example, follow these steps:

1. Create child.html using a text editor such as Windows WordPad.

2. Enter the following code.

```
<!DOCTYPE html>

<html>
  <head>
    <title>
      Child
    </title>

  </head>

  <body>
  </body>
</html>
```

3. Add the following code to create a <div> element that we'll use to display the text of the message we receive in child.html.

```
<!DOCTYPE html>

<html>
  <head>
    <title>
      Child
    </title>

  </head>

  <body>
    <div id="messages"  style="width:400px;
      height:250px"></div>
  </body>
</html>
```

4. Save child.html. Make sure you save this code in text format (the default format for WordPad, for example, is RTF, rich-text format, which won't work with browsers).

We've started child.html. Now let it receive the message.

Receiving a Cross-Window Message

Now let's enable child.html to receive and display the message sent to it by parent.html. To do that, follow these steps:

1. Open child.html using a text editor such as Windows WordPad.

2. Add the following code to connect the onMessage event to a function named loader().

```
<!DOCTYPE html>

<html>
  <head>
    <title>
      Child
    </title>

    <script type="text/javascript">
      window.addEventListener("message", loader,
        false);
    </script>

  </head>

  <body>
    <div id="messages"  style="width:400px;
      height:250px"></div>
  </body>
</html>
```

3. Add the following code to read the message from the event object's data property and display it in the <div> in child.html.

```
<!DOCTYPE html>

<html>
  <head>
    <title>
      Child
    </title>

    <script type="text/javascript">
      window.addEventListener("message", loader,
        false);
```

```
    function loader(e)
    {
      document.getElementById
        ("messages").innerHTML = e.data;
    }
  </script>

  </head>

  <body>
    <div id="messages"  style="width:400px;
      height:250px"></div>
  </body>
</html>
```

4. Save child.html. Make sure you save this code in text format (the default format for WordPad, for example, is RTF, rich-text format, which won't work with browsers).

Now, as shown in Figures 7.1 and 7.2, the user can open parent.html in a messaging-supported browser (Opera or Safari), enter text into the text field, click the button, and see the message sent to child.html appear. Cool.

The parent.html Example Code

Here is the whole parent.html example code:

```
<!DOCTYPE html>

<html>
  <head>
    <title>
      Cross-Window Messaging
    </title>

    <script type="text/javascript">
      function send()
      {
        var message =
          document.getElementById("message").value;
        var location = window.location;
        var protocol = location.protocol;
        var host = location.host;
```

```
            document.getElementById
              ("iframe").contentWindow.postMessage
                (message, protocol+"//"+host);
          }
        </script>
      </head>

      <body>
        <h1>Cross-Window Messaging</h1>
        <iframe id="iframe" src="child.html"
          height="300" width="600">
        </iframe>
        <br>
        <br>
        Message to Send: <input id="message"
          type="text">
        <input type="button" onclick="send();"
          value="Send">
      </body>
    </html>
```

The child.html Example Code

Here is the whole child.html example code:

```
<!DOCTYPE html>

<html>
  <head>
    <title>
      Child
    </title>

    <script type="text/javascript">
      window.addEventListener("message", loader,
        false);

      function loader(e)
      {
        document.getElementById
          ("messages").innerHTML = e.data;
      }
    </script>

  </head>
```

```
<body>
  <div id="messages"  style="width:400px;
    height:250px"></div>
</body>
</html>
```

Starting the domainparent.html Example

Now we'll see how cross-domain messaging works. To get started with the domainparent.html example, follow these steps:

1. Create domainparent.html using a text editor such as Windows WordPad.

2. Enter the following code.

```
<!DOCTYPE html>

<html>
  <head>
    <title>
      Cross-Domain Messaging
    </title>

  </head>

  <body>
    <h1>Cross-Domain Messaging</h1>
        .
        .
        .
</html>
```

3. Add the following code to create the <iframe> element this example uses to display domainchild.html in, as well as a text field to accept the message to send, and a button connected to a function named send() to send the message (replace *www.domain.com* with the domain where you're going to store domainchild.html).

```
<!DOCTYPE html>

<html>
  <head>
    <title>
      Cross-Domain Messaging
    </title>

  </head>

  <body>
    <h1>Cross-Domain Messaging</h1>
    <iframe id="iframe"
      src="http://www.domain.com/domainchild.html"
      height="300" width="600">
    </iframe>
    <br>
    <br>
    Message to Send: <input id="message"
      type="text">
    <input type="button" onclick="send();"
      value="Send">
  </body>
</html>
```

4. Save domainparent.html. Make sure you save this code in text format (the default format for WordPad, for example, is RTF, rich-text format, which won't work with browsers).

We've started domainparent.html. Now let's make it send the message.

Sending a Cross-Domain Message

You can send a cross-domain message from domainparent.html to domain-child.html; to do so, follow these steps:

1. Open domainparent.html using a text editor such as Windows WordPad.

2. Add the following code to implement the send() function that sends the message.

```
<!DOCTYPE html>

<html>
  <head>
```

```
<title>
  Cross-Domain Messaging
</title>

<script type="text/javascript">
  function send()
  {
     .
     .
     .
  }
</script>
</head>

<body>
  <h1>Cross-Domain Messaging</h1>
  <iframe id="iframe"
    src="http://www.domain.com/domainchild.html"
    height="300" width="600">
  </iframe>
  <br>
  <br>
  Message to Send: <input id="message"
    type="text">
  <input type="button" onclick="send();"
    value="Send">
</body>
</html>
```

3. Add the following code to send the message to the target window; this time, we'll use the full URL of the domainchild.html page, with an origin of "*"—which will work smoothly with any origin.

```
<!DOCTYPE html>

<html>
  <head>
    <title>
      Cross-Domain Messaging
    </title>

    <script type="text/javascript">
      function send()
      {
        var message =
```

```
        document.getElementById("message").value;
        document.getElementById
        ("iframe").contentWindow.postMessage
        (message, "*");
    }
    </script>
</head>

<body>
    <h1>Cross-Domain Messaging</h1>
    <iframe id="iframe"
        src="http://www.domain.com/domainchild.html"
        height="300" width="600">
    </iframe>
    <br>
    <br>
    Message to Send: <input id="message"
        type="text">
    <input type="button" onclick="send();"
        value="Send">
</body>
</html>
```

4. Save domainparent.html. Make sure you save this code in text
format (the default format for WordPad, for example, is RTF,
rich-text format, which won't work with browsers).

At this point, users can enter a message into the text field, as shown in
Figure 7.3. They can click the button to send the message to
domainchild.html, even though domainchild.html comes from a different
domain. Let's build domainchild.html next (don't try to run domainpar-
ent.html until you've completed domainchild.html).

Starting the domainchild.html
Example

To get started with the domainchild.html example, just follow these steps:

1. Create domainchild.html using a text editor such as Windows
WordPad.

2. Enter the following code.

```
<!DOCTYPE html>

<html>
  <head>
    <title>
      Child
    </title>

  </head>

  <body>
      .
      .
      .
  </body>
</html>
```

3. Add the following code to create a <div> element that we'll use to display the text of the message we receive in domainchild.html.

```
<!DOCTYPE html>

<html>
  <head>
    <title>
      Child
    </title>

  </head>

  <body>
    <div id="messages"  style="width:400px;
      height:250px"></div>
  </body>
</html>
```

4. Save domainchild.html at the domain you've chosen (replacing www.domain.com in domainparent.html with that domain). Make sure you save this code in text format (the default format for WordPad, for example, is RTF, rich-text format, which won't work with browsers).

We've begun domainchild.html. Now let's let it receive the message.

Receiving a Cross-Domain Message

At this point, we'll enable domainchild.html to receive the cross-domain message sent to it by domainparent.html. To do that, follow these steps:

1. Open domainchild.html using a text editor such as Windows WordPad.

2. Add the following code to connect the onMessage event to a function named loader().

    ```
    <!DOCTYPE html>

    <html>
      <head>
        <title>
          Child
        </title>

        <script type="text/javascript">
          window.addEventListener("message", loader,
            false);
            .
            .
            .
        </script>

      </head>

      <body>
        <div id="messages"  style="width:400px;
          height:250px"></div>
      </body>
    </html>
    ```

3. Add the following code to read the message from the event object's data property and display it in the <div> in domainchild.html.

    ```
    <!DOCTYPE html>

    <html>
      <head>
    ```

```
<title>
  Child
</title>

<script type="text/javascript">
  window.addEventListener("message", loader,
    false);

  function loader(e)
  {
    document.getElementById
      ("messages").innerHTML = e.data;
  }
</script>

</head>

<body>
  <div id="messages"  style="width:400px;
    height:250px"></div>
</body>
</html>
```

4. Save domainchild.html. Make sure you save this code in text format (the default format for WordPad, for example, is RTF, rich-text format, which won't work with browsers).

Now, as shown in Figures 7.3 and 7.4, the user can open domainparent.html in a supported browser (Opera or Safari), enter a message into the text field, click the button, and see the message sent cross-domain to domainchild.html appear.

The domainparent.html Example Code

Here is the whole domainpophistory.html example code—replace www.domain.com with the domain domainchild.html is at:

```
<!DOCTYPE html>

<html>
```

```
<head>
  <title>
    Cross-Domain Messaging
  </title>

  <script type="text/javascript">
    function send()
    {
      var message =
        document.getElementById("message").value;
      document.getElementById
        ("iframe").contentWindow.postMessage
          (message, "*");
    }
  </script>
</head>

<body>
  <h1>Cross-Domain Messaging</h1>
  <iframe id="iframe"
    src="http://www.domain.com/domainchild.html"
    height="300" width="600">
  </iframe>
  <br>
  <br>
  Message to Send: <input id="message"
    type="text">
  <input type="button" onclick="send();"
    value="Send">
</body>
</html>
```

The domainchild.html Example Code

Here is the whole domainchild.html example code:

```
<!DOCTYPE html>

<html>
  <head>
    <title>
      Child
```

```
    </title>

    <script type="text/javascript">
      window.addEventListener("message", loader,
        false);

      function loader(e)
      {
        document.getElementById
          ("messages").innerHTML = e.data;
      }
    </script>

  </head>

  <body>
    <div id="messages"  style="width:400px;
      height:250px"></div>
  </body>
</html>
```

LESSON 8

Using Video and Audio

HTML5 lets you play video with ease—just use the <video> element.

Currently, however, most browsers that let you play video only play videos in .ogg format, a relatively obscure open-source format. Fortunately, you can convert videos from almost any format into .ogg format. In addition, some browsers enable you to use other video formats with the <video> element.

In this lesson, we'll play an .ogg video in an HTML5 web page, including displaying controls so the user can control playback.

We'll also take a look at playing audio in this lesson with the new <audio> element.

> TIP: One reason the <video> element is so eagerly anticipated is because the Apple iPad does not play Flash video, and the <video> element may supplant it.

Welcome to the Video Media Control

In this lesson, we'll develop an example named video.html, which you can see in Figure 8.1. This example plays a video named hawaii.ogg, which is included in the download for this book.

Let's look at some of the details behind this example now.

FIGURE 8.1   The video.html example.

Getting to Know the Video Element API

The <video> element has a number of attributes; here are the details:

Element:

 ▶ <video>

Attributes:

 ▶ autoplay

 ▶ controls

 ▶ height

 ▶ loop

- poster
- preload
- src
- width
- onerror

Supported browsers:

- Chrome, Opera, Firefox, Safari, Internet Explorer 9

You can read what the W3C has to say about the <video> element at www.w3.org/TR/html5/video.html.

Let's take a look at the attributes in overview next.

The autoplay Attribute

The autoplay attribute is a true/false attribute that controls whether the video plays automatically.

The controls Attribute

The controls attribute lets you specify whether to display a control bar under the video with play/pause buttons.

The height Attribute

This attribute sets the height of the video.

The loop Attribute

The loop attribute is a true/false attribute that, if true, makes the video play over and over.

The poster Attribute

This attribute holds the URL of an image to display if no video is available.

The preload Attribute

The preload attribute controls whether the video is preloaded into the <video> element; it can take one of three values:

▶ none—No preloading necessary.

▶ metadata—Tells the browser that detecting metadata about the video (dimensions, first frame, and so on) is a good idea.

▶ auto—The browser can decide whether to preload the video.

The src Attribute

The src attribute holds the URL of the video.

The width Attribute

The width attribute specifies the width of the video.

In this lesson, we'll see the <video> element at work as it plays .ogg videos, and we'll start by seeing how to convert from common video formats to .ogg format.

The onerror Attribute

The <video> element has an error event that occurs when there is a failure.

Converting to OGG Format

At this point, most browsers can only use the <video> element to play .ogg format video (although more formats are coming). Being able to play OGG format videos is all very well, but what if your video is in .wmv format? Or .mp4?

First, you might check if your browser supports your current format by specifying the URL of your video in the src attribute of a <video> element. As time goes on, more browsers will display more video formats.

But if you find you have to stick with OGG format, it's time to find a file convertor, like the one at http://media-convert.com/. This popular file convertor appears in Figure 8.2. It's popular because it converts from many file formats to many others, and because it's online, there's nothing to download.

FIGURE 8.2   The media-convert.com site.

Do you want to convert a video to OGG format using this site? Just follow these steps:

1. Navigate to http://media-convert.com/.

2. Click the Browse button. A dialog box listing files appears.

3. Browse to the file you want to convert to OGG format and select it.

4. Click the Open button. The dialog box closes.

5. Select the format of your file in the Input Format box. There are many types to select from; for video formats, you can select and convert from these types:

- 3GP/3G2 Video (.3g2,.3gp)
- AMV Video Format (.amv)
- Apple QuickTime (.mov)
- ASF Video (.asf)
- Audio Video Interleave (.avi)
- Digital Video File (.dv)
- DPG Video (.dpg)
- DVD Video Object (.vob)
- Flash SWF (.swf)
- Flash Video (.flv)
- FLIC Animation (.fli)
- Google Video File (.gvi)
- Matroska (.mkv)
- MPEG 1 (.mpg)
- MPEG-2 (.mpg)
- MPEG-4 (.mp4)
- NSV (.nsv)
- OGG video (.ogg)
- Ogg Vorbis compressed video (.ogm)
- RealVideo (.rm)
- RPL video (.rpl)
- Video stream descriptor (.asx)
- Windows Media Video (.wmv)

6. Select the OGG Video (.ogg) item in the Output Format box.

7. Click the OK button.

The site converts your file and displays a URL to the completed OGG file. Use your browser to download the OGG file, and store it in the same directory as your page that uses the .ogg file.

Now that you have OGG files to work with, we can start on this lesson's example, video.html.

Starting the video.html Example

To get started with the video.html example, follow these steps:

1. Create video.html using a text editor such as Windows WordPad.

2. Enter the following code:

```
<!DOCTYPE html>

<html>
  <head>
    <title>
      HTML 5 Video
    </title>
  </head>

</html>
```

3. Add the following code to create the <body> element.

```
<!DOCTYPE html>

<html>
  <head>
    <title>
      HTML 5 Video
    </title>
  </head>

  <body>
    <h1>HTML 5 Video</h1>
         .
         .
         .
  </body>
</html>
```

4. Save video.html. Make sure you save this code in text format (the default format for WordPad, for example, is RTF, rich-text format, which won't work with browsers).

We've started video.html; now let's make it do something.

To add the <video> element to the video.html example, follow these steps:

1. Open video.html using a text editor such as Windows WordPad.

2. Enter the following code:

```
<!DOCTYPE html>

<html>
  <head>
    <title>
      HTML 5 Video
    </title>
  </head>

  <body>
    <h1>HTML 5 Video</h1>
    <video>
    </video>
  </body>
</html>
```

3. Add the following code to specify the location of the video and its dimensions:

```
<!DOCTYPE html>

<html>
  <head>
    <title>
      HTML 5 Video
    </title>
  </head>

  <body>
    <h1>HTML 5 Video</h1>
    <video height="300" width="400"
      src="hawaii.ogg">
    </video>
  </body>
</html>
```

4. Save video.html in the same directory as your .ogg video. Make sure you save this code in text format (the default format for

WordPad, for example, is RTF, rich-text format, which won't work with browsers).

That displays the video, but the only way to play it is to right-click it and select the Play item. In the next task, we'll make it easier to play by displaying controls.

Adding Controls to the video.html Example

To add video controls to the video.html example, follow these steps:

1. Open video.html using a text editor such as Windows WordPad.

2. Enter the controls attribute to the <video> element.

```
<!DOCTYPE html>

<html>
  <head>
    <title>
      HTML 5 Video
    </title>
  </head>

  <body>
    <h1>HTML 5 Video</h1>
    <video controls height="300" width="400"
      src="hawaii.ogg">
    </video>
  </body>
</html>
```

3. Save video.html. Make sure you save this code in text format (the default format for WordPad, for example, is RTF, rich-text format, which won't work with browsers).

Now the video appears as shown in Figure 8.1. To play the video, click the Play button. Cool.

Looping a Video

You can make a video loop over and over; to do so follow these steps:

1. Open video.html using a text editor such as Windows WordPad.

2. Enter the following code:

```
<!DOCTYPE html>

<html>
  <head>
    <title>
      HTML 5 Video
    </title>
  </head>

  <body>
    <h1>HTML 5 Video</h1>
    <video controls height="300" width="400"
      loop src="hawaii.ogg">
    </video>
  </body>
</html>
```

3. Save video.html. Make sure you save this code in text format (the default format for WordPad, for example, is RTF, rich-text format, which won't work with browsers).

Now when the user plays the video, it'll loop continuously.

Playing a Video Automatically

You can make a video play automatically when its page opens; to do so, follow these steps:

1. Open video.html using a text editor such as Windows WordPad.

2. Enter the following code:

```
<!DOCTYPE html>

<html>
```

```
<head>
  <title>
    HTML 5 Video
  </title>
</head>

<body>
  <h1>HTML 5 Video</h1>
  <video controls height="300" width="400"
    autoplay src="hawaii.ogg">
  </video>
</body>
</html>
```

3. Save video.html. Make sure you save this code in text format (the default format for WordPad, for example, is RTF, rich-text format, which won't work with browsers).

Detecting When a Video Has Failed

You can catch video failures with the onerror attribute, handling several different errors (such as not being able to find the video). Here's how:

1. Open video.html using a text editor such as Windows WordPad.

2. Enter the following JavaScript code to create the fail() function, handle the possible errors, and alert the user.

```
<!DOCTYPE html>

<html>
  <head>
    <title>
      HTML 5 Video
    </title>

    <script>
      function fail(e)
      {
        switch (e.target.error.code) {
```

```
        case e.target.error.MEDIA_ERR_ABORTED:
            alert('You aborted the playback.');
            break;
        case e.target.error.MEDIA_ERR_NETWORK:
            alert('Network error.');
            break;
        case e.target.error.MEDIA_ERR_DECODE:
            alert('Corruption problem.');
            break;
        case
      e.target.error.MEDIA_ERR_SRC_NOT_SUPPORTED:
            alert(
            'Format unsupported or file not found.');
            break;
        default:
            alert('An unknown error occurred.');
            break;
        }
      }
    </script>
  </head>

  <body>
    <h1>HTML 5 Video</h1>
    <video controls height="300" width="400"
      src="hawaii.ogg">
    </video>
  </body>
</html>
```

3. Enter the following code to connect the fail() function to the
   <video> element.

```
<!DOCTYPE html>

<html>
  <head>
    <title>
      HTML 5 Video
    </title>

    <script>
      function fail(e)
      {
        switch (e.target.error.code) {
```

```
          case e.target.error.MEDIA_ERR_ABORTED:
            alert('You aborted the playback.');
            break;
          case e.target.error.MEDIA_ERR_NETWORK:
            alert('Network error.');
            break;
          case e.target.error.MEDIA_ERR_DECODE:
            alert('Corruption problem.');
            break;
          case
        e.target.error.MEDIA_ERR_SRC_NOT_SUPPORTED:
            alert(
            'Format unsupported or file not found.');
            break;
          default:
            alert('An unknown error occurred.');
            break;
        }
      }
    </script>
  </head>

  <body>
    <h1>HTML 5 Video</h1>
    <video controls height="300" width="400"
      onerror="fail(event)" src="hawaii.ogg">
    </video>
  </body>
</html>
```

4. Save video.html. Make sure you save this code in text format (the
default format for WordPad, for example, is RTF, rich-text format, which won't work with browsers).

Now when an error occurs, the page will inform the user, as shown in
Figure 8.3.

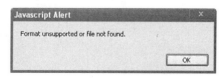

FIGURE 8.3   A video error.

Welcome to the Audio Media Control

Next, we'll develop an example named audio.html, which you can see in Figure 8.4.

FIGURE 8.4 The audio.html example.

If you want to play the audio, just click the Play button. As with the <video> element, most browsers let you play .ogg audio (other formats are coming). If you need to onvert to .ogg format, you can use media-convert.com.

Let's see some of the details behind this example now.

Getting to Know the Audio Element API

The <audio> element has a number of attributes available for use; here are the details:

Element:

▶ <audio>

Attributes:

▶ autoplay

▶ controls

- ▶ loop

- ▶ preload

- ▶ src

- ▶ onerror

Supported browsers:

- ▶ Chrome. Opera, Safari, Firefox, Internet Explorer 9

You can read what the W3C has to say about the <audio> element at:
http://www.w3.org/TR/html5/video.html#audio.

We'll take a look at the attributes in overview next.

The autoplay Attribute

As with the <video> element, the autoplay attribute is a true/false attribute
that controls whether the audio plays automatically.

The controls Attribute

The controls attribute lets you specify whether to display a control bar
with play/pause buttons so the user can control playback.

The loop Attribute

The loop attribute is a true/false attribute that, if true, makes the audio play
over and over.

The preload Attribute

As with the <video> control, the preload attribute controls whether the
audio is preloaded into the page. It can take one of these three values:

- ▶ none—No preloading necessary.

- ▶ metadata—Tells the browser that detecting metadata about the
  audio (length, etc.) is a good idea.

- ▶ auto—The browser can decide whether to preload the audio.

The src Attribute

The src attribute holds the URL of the sound file you want to play.

The onerror Attribute

The <audio> element has an error event that occurs when there is a failure, as when the sound file is not found.

Starting the audio.html Example

To get started with the audio.html example, follow these steps:

1. Create audio.html using a text editor such as Windows WordPad.

2. Enter the following code:

```
<!DOCTYPE html>

<html>
  <head>
    <title>
       HTML 5 Audio
    </title>
  </head>
         .
         .
         .
  </html>
```

3. Add the following code to create the <body> element:

```
<!DOCTYPE html>

<html>
  <head>
    <title>
       HTML 5 Audio
    </title>
  </head>

  <body>
    <h1>HTML 5 Audio</h1>
         .
```

```
        .
        .
   </body>
  </html>
```

4. Save audio.html. Make sure you save this code in text format (the
   default format for WordPad, for example, is RTF, rich-text format, which won't work with browsers).

We've started audio.html. Now let's make it do something.

To add the <audio> element to the audio.html example, follow these steps:

1. Open audio.html using a text editor such as Windows WordPad.

2. Enter the following code:

```
<!DOCTYPE html>

<html>
  <head>
    <title>
      HTML 5 Audio
    </title>
  </head>

  <body>
    <h1>HTML 5 Audio</h1>
    <audio>
    </audio>
  </body>
</html>
```

3. Add the following code to specify the location of the audio and
   to add controls so the user can play the sound recording.

```
<!DOCTYPE html>

<html>
  <head>
    <title>
      HTML 5 Audio
    </title>
  </head>
```

```
<body>
  <h1>HTML 5 Audio</h1>
  <audio controls src="hawaii.ogg">
  </audio>
</body>
</html>
```

4. Save audio.html. Make sure you save this code in text format (the default format for WordPad, for example, is RTF, rich-text format, which won't work with browsers).

There you have it—now the user can click the Play button to play the sound recording.

As with the <video> element, you can use the loop attribute to make the playback keep repeating, and use the autoplay attribute to make the sound start as soon as the page loads.

> TIP: Note that it's possible, if you omit the controls attribute and include the autoplay and loop attributes, to create one of those annoying pages that play music continuously as soon as it loads with no way to turn it off—but it's not going to make your users like you very much.

Detecting When an Audio Has Failed

You can catch audio failures with the onerror attribute, handling several different errors; here's how:

1. Open audio.html using a text editor such as Windows WordPad.

2. Enter the following JavaScript code to create the fail() function, handle the possible errors, and alert the user.

```
<!DOCTYPE html>

<html>
  <head>
    <title>
```

```
        HTML 5 Audio
      </title>

      <script>
        function fail(e)
        {
          switch (e.target.error.code) {
            case e.target.error.MEDIA_ERR_ABORTED:
              alert('You aborted the playback.');
              break;
            case e.target.error.MEDIA_ERR_NETWORK:
              alert('Network error.');
              break;
            case e.target.error.MEDIA_ERR_DECODE:
              alert('Corruption problem.');
              break;
            case
          e.target.error.MEDIA_ERR_SRC_NOT_SUPPORTED:
              alert(
              'Format unsupported or file not found.');
              break;
            default:
              alert('An unknown error occurred.');
              break;
          }
        }
      </script>
    </head>

  <body>
    <h1>HTML 5 Audio</h1>
    <audio controls
      src="hawaii.ogg">
    </audio>
  </body>
</html>
```

3. Enter the following code to connect the fail() function to the
   <audio> element.

```
<!DOCTYPE html>

<html>
  <head>
    <title>
```

```
       HTML 5 Audio
       </title>

       <script>
         function fail(e)
         {
           switch (e.target.error.code) {
             case e.target.error.MEDIA_ERR_ABORTED:
               alert('You aborted the playback.');
               break;
             case e.target.error.MEDIA_ERR_NETWORK:
               alert('Network error.');
               break;
             case e.target.error.MEDIA_ERR_DECODE:
               alert('Corruption problem.');
               break;
             case
         e.target.error.MEDIA_ERR_SRC_NOT_SUPPORTED:
               alert(
               'Format unsupported or file not found.');
               break;
             default:
               alert('An unknown error occurred.');
               break;
           }
         }
       </script>
       </head>

       <body>
         <h1>HTML 5 Audio</h1>
         <audio controls
           onerror="fail(event)" src="hawaii.ogg">
         </audio>
       </body>
       </html>
```

4. Save audio.html. Make sure you save this code in text format (the default format for WordPad, for example, is RTF, rich-text format, which won't work with browsers).

Now when there's an error, the page will inform the user.

LESSON 9

Web Storage

One of the things that HTML authors have missed is some way of storing data between page accesses. When the page gets refreshed, all JavaScript variables get reset to their original values, for example. How can you store data that's still there when the user comes back to your page?

This is often why people start working with server-side code—to preserve data between page accesses. However, now, in HTML5, there's a new way. So, for example, if you're keeping track of a user's purchases, you can store that information so that it'll be available when they come back to the page.

Using plain JavaScript and HTML5, you can now store data so that it's there even after the current page is reloaded. You can store data in either the current browser session with the server (data is usually deleted after 15 minutes of user inactivity) or locally, in the browser. We'll take a look at both ways in this lesson, starting with session storage.

Welcome to Session Storage

When a browser connects to a server, it starts a session. The browser can store data in that session, and that data will be safe as long as there isn't 15 minutes of inactivity on the user's part. If there is, the session times out and the session data is deleted.

In this lesson, we'll create an example called sessionstorage.html, which appears in Figure 9.1.

The user can enter some data into the text field, as shown in Figure 9.1, and click the Store button to store that data in the session. Then the user can erase the data from the text field, as shown in Figure 9.2.

FIGURE 9.1   The sessionstorage.html example.

FIGURE 9.2   Erasing data.

Then you can click the Get button to get the stored data from the session, as shown in Figure 9.3.

In other words, the sessionstorage.html example shows you how to save and get data from the session, using only JavaScript.

Note that to use this example, the browser must be talking to a web server, which means that you have to upload sessionstorage.html to a web server and open it in your browser. You can't just open it from your disk and have it work.

FIGURE 9.3   Getting data back again.

Getting to Know the Session Storage API

Session storage is based on the JavaScript object named sessionStorage, which comes built in to browsers that support this HTML5 feature. You can read about this object at: http://dev.w3.org/html5/webstorage/. Here are the details:

Object:

▶ sessionStorage

Attributes:

▶ length attribute

Functions:

▶ key() function

▶ getItem() function

▶ setItem() function

▶ removeItem() function

▶ clear() function

Supported browsers:

▶ Firefox and Safari

You store values in the sessionStorage object using key/value pairs—that is, when you store data, you specify both the data and the key (text like "data" or "phone"). When you read data back, you supply the key.

Let's take a look at the sessionStorage object's attributes and functions now.

The length Attribute

The length attribute holds the number of key/value pairs currently present in the sessionStorage object.

The key() Function

Here's how you use this function:

▶ key(index)

This function returns the name of the nth key in the sessionStorage object.

The getItem() Function

Here's how you use this function:

▶ getItem(key)

This function returns the value of the item associated with the specified key.

The setItem() Function

Here's how you use this function:

▶ setItem(key, data)

You use this function to store data in the session. You specify the key to store data under, and the value of that data. For example, setItem("Data", "turbulent") stores the word "turbulent" under the key "Data".

The removeItem() Function

Here's how you use this function:

▶ removeItem(key)

You use this function to remove items from the sessionStorage object.

The clear() Function

The clear() function clears all session data.

Now let's put all this to work in the sessionstorage.html example, where we store and then get data from the session.

Starting the sessionstorage.html Example

To get started with the sessionstorage.html example, follow these steps:

1. Create sessionstorage.html using a text editor such as Windows WordPad.

2. Enter the following code.

```
<!DOCTYPE html>
<html>
  <head>
    <title>
      Web Storage
    </title>
  </head>

  <body>
    <h1>Session Storage</h1>
      .
      .
      .
  </body>
</html>
```

3. Add the following code to create the text field and the three buttons.

```
<!DOCTYPE html>
<html>
  <head>
    <title>
      Web Storage
    </title>
  </head>

  <body>
    <h1>Session Storage</h1>
    Data <input id="Data" type="text">
    <input type="button" value="Store">
    <input type="button" value="Get">
    <input type="button" value="Clear">
  </body>
</html>
```

4. Save sessionstorage.html. Make sure you save this code in text format (the default format for WordPad, for example, is RTF, rich-text format, which won't work with browsers).

We've started sessionstorage.html; now let's make it do something.

Storing Data in the Session

To store the data the user enters in the sessionstorage.html example, follow these steps:

1. Open sessionstorage.html using a text editor such as Windows WordPad.

2. Enter the following code to connect the Store button to JavaScript.

```
<!DOCTYPE html>
<html>
  <head>
    <title>
      Web Storage
    </title>
  </head>

  <body>
    <h1>Session Storage</h1>
```

```
  Data <input id="Data" type="text">
  <input type="button" value="Store"
    onclick="sessionStore();">
  <input type="button" value="Get">
  <input type="button" value="Clear">
  </body>
</html>
```

3. Add the following code to read the text the user has entered and store it in the session.

```
<!DOCTYPE html>
<html>
  <head>
    <title>
      Web Storage
    </title>
    <script type="text/javascript">
    function sessionStore()
    {
      var text =
        document.getElementById
        ("Data").value;
      sessionStorage.setItem("Data", text);
    }
    </script>
  </head>

<body>
  <h1>Session Storage</h1>
  Data <input id="Data" type="text">
  <input type="button" value="Store"
    onclick="sessionStore();">
  <input type="button" value="Get"
    onclick="sessionGet();">
  <input type="button" value="Clear"
    onclick="sessionClear();">
  </body>
</html>
```

4. Save sessionstorage.html. Make sure you save this code in text format (the default format for WordPad, for example, is RTF, rich-text format, which won't work with browsers).

That stores the data the user has entered in the session. Now how about getting it back?

Getting Data from the Session

To get the stored data back from the session in the sessionstorage.html example, follow these steps:

1. Open sessionstorage.html using a text editor such as Windows WordPad.

2. Enter the following code to connect the Get button to JavaScript.

```
<!DOCTYPE html>
<html>
  <head>
    <title>
      Web Storage
    </title>
    <script type="text/javascript">
      function sessionStore()
      {
        var text =
          document.getElementById
          ("Data").value;
        sessionStorage.setItem("Data", text);
      }
    </script>
  </head>

  <body>
    <h1>Session Storage</h1>
    Data <input id="Data" type="text">
    <input type="button" value="Store"
      onclick="sessionStore();">
    <input type="button" value="Get"
      onclick="sessionGet();">
    <input type="button" value="Clear">
  </body>
</html>
```

3. Add the following code to read the data from the session and display it in the text field again.

```
<!DOCTYPE html>
<html>
  <head>
    <title>
      Web Storage
    </title>
```

```
<script type="text/javascript">
function sessionStore()
{
  var text =
    document.getElementById
    ("Data").value;
  sessionStorage.setItem("Data", text);
}

function sessionGet()
{
  document.getElementById("Data").value =
    sessionStorage.getItem("Data");
}
</script>
</head>

<body>
  <h1>Session Storage</h1>
  Data <input id="Data" type="text">
  <input type="button" value="Store"
    onclick="sessionStore();">
  <input type="button" value="Get"
    onclick="sessionGet();">
  <input type="button" value="Clear"
    onclick="sessionClear();">
</body>
</html>
```

4. Save sessionstorage.html. Make sure you save this code in text format (the default format for WordPad, for example, is RTF, rich-text format, which won't work with browsers).

That restores the data from the session.

Clearing Session Data

You can also clear the data in the session; to do so, follow these steps:

1. Open sessionstorage.html using a text editor such as Windows WordPad.

2. Enter the following code to connect the Clear button to JavaScript.

```
<!DOCTYPE html>
<html>
  <head>
    <title>
      Web Storage
    </title>
    <script type="text/javascript">
    function sessionStore()
    {
      var text =
        document.getElementById
        ("Data").value;
        sessionStorage.setItem("Data", text);
    }

    function sessionGet()
    {
      document.getElementById("Data").value =
        sessionStorage.getItem("Data");
    }
    </script>
  </head>

  <body>
    <h1>Session Storage</h1>
    Data <input id="Data" type="text">
    <input type="button" value="Store"
      onclick="sessionStore();">
    <input type="button" value="Get"
      onclick="sessionGet();">
    <input type="button" value="Clear"
      onclick="sessionClear();">
  </body>
</html>
```

3. Add the following code to clear the session data.

```
<!DOCTYPE html>
<html>
  <head>
    <title>
      Web Storage
    </title>
    <script type="text/javascript">
    function sessionStore()
    {
      var text =
```

```
      document.getElementById
      ("Data").value;
      sessionStorage.setItem("Data", text);
    }

    function sessionGet()
    {
      document.getElementById("Data").value =
      sessionStorage.getItem("Data");
    }

    function sessionClear()
    {
      sessionStorage.removeItem("Data");
      document.getElementById("Data").value =
      "";
    }
  </script>
</head>

<body>
  <h1>Session Storage</h1>
  Data <input id="Data" type="text">
  <input type="button" value="Store"
    onclick="sessionStore();">
  <input type="button" value="Get"
    onclick="sessionGet();">
  <input type="button" value="Clear"
    onclick="sessionClear();">
</body>
</html>
```

4. Save sessionstorage.html. Make sure you save this code in text format (the default format for WordPad, for example, is RTF, rich-text format, which won't work with browsers).

And now you can clear the data in the session.

The sessionstorage.html Code

For reference, here is the full sessionstorage.html code:

```
<!DOCTYPE html>
<html>
```

```
<head>
  <title>
    Web Storage
  </title>
  <script type="text/javascript">
    function sessionStore()
    {
      var text =
        document.getElementById
        ("Data").value;
      sessionStorage.setItem("Data", text);
    }

    function sessionGet()
    {
      document.getElementById("Data").value =
        sessionStorage.getItem("Data");
    }

    function sessionClear()
    {
      sessionStorage.removeItem("Data");
      document.getElementById("Data").value =
        "";
    }
  </script>
</head>

<body>
  <h1>Session Storage</h1>
  Data <input id="Data" type="text">
  <input type="button" value="Store"
    onclick="sessionStore();">
  <input type="button" value="Get"
    onclick="sessionGet();">
  <input type="button" value="Clear"
    onclick="sessionClear();">
</body>
</html>
```

Welcome to Local Storage

Besides storing data in a server-side session, you can store data in the
browser. In this lesson, we'll create an example called localstorage.html,
which appears in Figure 9.4.

FIGURE 9.4   The localstorage.html example.

As with the sessionstorage.html example, you can enter some text into the
text field, as shown in Figure 9.4, and click the Store button to store that
data in the browser. Then you can erase the data from the text field, as
shown in Figure 9.5.

FIGURE 9.5   Erasing data.

Then you can click the Get button to get the stored data from the browser,
as shown in Figure 9.6.

The localstorage.html example shows you how to save and get data from
the browser between page accesses, using only JavaScript.

FIGURE 9.6   Getting data back again.

Getting to Know the Local Storage API

You can also use local storage in the browser, which is good until the user closes the browser. That is, the user can come back to the same page over and over, and the data will still be available as long as the user hasn't closed the browser.

Local storage revolves around the localSession object. You can read about this object at: http://dev.w3.org/html5/webstorage/. Here are the details:

Object:

► localStorage

Attributes:

► length attribute

Functions:

► key() function

► getItem() function

► setItem() function

► removeItem() function

► clear() function

Supported Browsers:

► Chrome, Firefox and Safari

As with the sessionStorage object earlier in this lesson, you store values in the localStorage object using key/value pairs—that is, when you store data, you specify both the data and the key. When you read data back, you supply the key.

For the details on how to use these attributes and functions, take a look at the sessionStorage object's section at the beginning of this lesson. The syntax is the same for the attributes and functions of localStorage.

Starting the localstorage.html Example

To get started with the localstorage.html example, follow these steps:

1. Create localstorage.html using a text editor such as Windows WordPad.

2. Enter the following code:

```
<!DOCTYPE html>
<html>
  <head>
    <title>
      Web Storage
    </title>
  </head>

  <body>
    <h1>Local Storage</h1>
       .
       .
       .
  </body>
</html>
```

3. Add the following code to create the text field and the three
buttons:

```
<!DOCTYPE html>
<html>
  <head>
    <title>
      Web Storage
    </title>
  </head>

  <body>
    <h1>Local Storage</h1>
    Data <input id="Data" type="text">
    <input type="button" value="Store">
    <input type="button" value="Get">
    <input type="button" value="Clear">
  </body>
</html>
```

4. Save localstorage.html. Make sure you save this code in text format (the default format for WordPad, for example, is RTF, rich-
text format, which won't work with browsers).

We've started localstorage.html; now let's make it do something.

Storing Data in the Browser

To store the data the user enters in the localstorage.html example, follow
these steps:

1. Open localstorage.html using a text editor such as Windows
WordPad.

2. Enter the following code to connect the Store button to
JavaScript.

```
<!DOCTYPE html>
<html>
  <head>
    <title>
      Web Storage
    </title>
  </head>
```

```
<body>
  <h1>Local Storage</h1>
  Data <input id="Data" type="text">
  <input type="button" value="Store"
    onclick="localStore();">
  <input type="button" value="Get">
  <input type="button" value="Clear">
</body>
</html>
```

3. Add the following code to read the text the user has entered and store it in the browser.

```
<!DOCTYPE html>
<html>
  <head>
    <title>
      Web Storage
    </title>
    <script type="text/javascript">
    function localStore()
    {
      var text =
        document.getElementById
        ("Data").value;
      localStorage.setItem("Data", text);
    }
    </script>
  </head>

  <body>
    <h1>Local Storage</h1>
    Data <input id="Data" type="text">
    <input type="button" value="Store"
      onclick="localStore();">
    <input type="button" value="Get"
      onclick="localGet();">
    <input type="button" value="Clear"
      onclick="localClear();">
  </body>
</html>
```

4. Save localstorage.html. Make sure you save this code in text format (the default format for WordPad, for example, is RTF, rich-text format, which won't work with browsers).

That stores the data the user has entered. Now how about getting it back from the browser?

Getting Data from the Browser

To get the stored data back from the browser in the localstorage.html example, follow these steps:

1. Open localstorage.html using a text editor such as Windows WordPad.

2. Enter the following code to connect the Get button to JavaScript:

```
<!DOCTYPE html>
<html>
  <head>
    <title>
      Web Storage
    </title>
    <script type="text/javascript">
      function localStore()
      {
        var text =
          document.getElementById
          ("Data").value;
        localStorage.setItem("Data", text);
      }
    </script>
  </head>

  <body>
    <h1>Local Storage</h1>
    Data <input id="Data" type="text">
    <input type="button" value="Store"
      onclick="localStore();">
    <input type="button" value="Get"
      onclick="localGet();">
    <input type="button" value="Clear">
  </body>
</html>
```

3. Add the following code to read the data from the local storage and display it in the text field again.

```
<!DOCTYPE html>
<html>
  <head>
    <title>
      Web Storage
    </title>
    <script type="text/javascript">
      function localStore()
      {
        var text =
          document.getElementById
          ("Data").value;
        localStorage.setItem("Data", text);
      }

      function localGet()
      {
        document.getElementById("Data").value =
          localStorage.getItem("Data");
      }
    </script>
  </head>

  <body>
    <h1>Local Storage</h1>
    Data <input id="Data" type="text">
    <input type="button" value="Store"
      onclick="localStore();">
    <input type="button" value="Get"
      onclick="localGet();">
    <input type="button" value="Clear"
      onclick="localClear();">
  </body>
</html>
```

4. Save localstorage.html. Make sure you save this code in text format (the default format for WordPad, for example, is RTF, rich-
   text format, which won't work with browsers).

And that reads the data back from the browser.

Clearing Local Data

You can also clear the data in the browser by following these steps:

1. Open localstorage.html using a text editor such as Windows WordPad.

2. Enter the following code to connect the Clear button to JavaScript:

```
<!DOCTYPE html>
<html>
  <head>
    <title>
      Web Storage
    </title>
    <script type="text/javascript">
      function localStore()
      {
        var text =
          document.getElementById
          ("Data").value;
        localStorage.setItem("Data", text);
      }

      function localGet()
      {
        document.getElementById("Data").value =
          localStorage.getItem("Data");
      }
    </script>
  </head>

  <body>
    <h1>Local Storage</h1>
    Data <input id="Data" type="text">
    <input type="button" value="Store"
      onclick="localStore();">
    <input type="button" value="Get"
      onclick="localGet();">
    <input type="button" value="Clear"
      onclick="localClear();">
  </body>
</html>
```

3. Add the following code to clear the local data:

```html
<!DOCTYPE html>
<html>
  <head>
    <title>
      Web Storage
    </title>
    <script type="text/javascript">
      function localStore()
      {
          var text =
          document.getElementById
          ("Data").value;
          localStorage.setItem("Data", text);
      }

      function localGet()
      {
          document.getElementById("Data").value =
          localStorage.getItem("Data");
      }

      function localClear()
      {
          localStorage.removeItem("Data");
          document.getElementById("Data").value =
          "";
      }
    </script>
  </head>

  <body>
    <h1>Local Storage</h1>
    Data <input id="Data" type="text">
    <input type="button" value="Store"
      onclick="localStore();">
    <input type="button" value="Get"
      onclick="localGet();">
    <input type="button" value="Clear"
      onclick="localClear();">
  </body>
</html>
```

4. Save localstorage.html. Make sure you save this code in text format (the default format for WordPad, for example, is RTF, rich-text format, which won't work with browsers).

That's how to clear the data you've stored in the browser.

The localstorage.html Code

For reference, here is the full localstorage.html code:

```
<!DOCTYPE html>
<html>
  <head>
    <title>
      Web Storage
    </title>
    <script type="text/javascript">
      function localStore()
      {
        var text =
          document.getElementById
          ("Data").value;
        localStorage.setItem("Data", text);
      }

      function localGet()
      {
        document.getElementById("Data").value =
          localStorage.getItem("Data");
      }

      function localClear()
      {
        localStorage.removeItem("Data");
        document.getElementById("Data").value =
        "";
      }
    </script>
  </head>

  <body>
    <h1>Local Storage</h1>
    Data <input id="Data" type="text">
```

```
<input type="button" value="Store"
  onclick="localStore();">
<input type="button" value="Get"
  onclick="localGet();">
<input type="button" value="Clear"
  onclick="localClear();">
</body>
</html>
```

LESSON 10

The New HTML5 Elements

HTML5 includes some new elements, and they're the focus of this lesson. We've already covered some of these new elements in previous lessons, but there are many more, most having to do with document structure.

Adding SVG and MathML

Here's something that might surprise you—HTML5 has taken two XML languages, SVG (Scalable Vector Graphics) and MathML (a language for displaying equations), and now supports them.

SVG is already supported by some browsers, such as Firefox, as you can see in Figure 10.1.

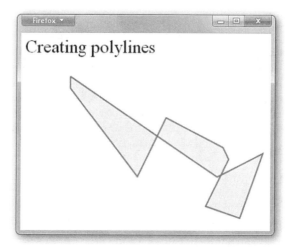

FIGURE 10.1   An SVG example.

Only one browser supports MathML and HTML at this time—that's the Amaya test browser from W3C, and you can get it at www.w3.org/ Amaya/.

Welcome to the New Elements

Here are the HTML elements that are new in HTML5:

- ▶ <article>
- ▶ <aside>
- ▶ <audio>
- ▶ <canvas>
- ▶ <command>
- ▶ <datalist>
- ▶ <details>
- ▶ <embed>
- ▶ <figcaption>
- ▶ <figure>
- ▶ <footer>
- ▶ <header>
- ▶ <hgroup>
- ▶ <keygen>
- ▶ <mark>
- ▶ <meter>
- ▶ <nav>
- ▶ <output>
- ▶ <progress>
- ▶ <rp>

- ► <rt>

- ► <ruby>

- ► <section>

- ► <source>

- ► <summary>

- ► <time>

- ► <video>

You can have a look at what W3C has to say about each of these elements at www.w3.org/TR/html5/spec.html#auto-toc-8. You should also take note that the following elements are dropped in HTML5:

- ► <acronym>

- ► <applet>

- ► <basefont>

- ► <big>

- ► <center>

- ► <dir>

- ► <font>

- ► <frame>

- ► <frameset>

- ► <isindex>

- ► <noframes>

- ► <s>

- ► <strike>

- ► <tt>

- ► <u>

Let's take a look at the new elements.

The <article> Element

The <article> element straddles an article, which is intended to be an independently distributable document, like an article in a magazine. Here are this element's attributes:

- ▶ accesskey
- ▶ class
- ▶ contenteditable
- ▶ contextmenu
- ▶ dir
- ▶ draggable
- ▶ hidden
- ▶ id
- ▶ lang
- ▶ spellcheck
- ▶ style
- ▶ tabindex
- ▶ title

Here's an example putting the <article> element to work:

```
<!DOCTYPE HTML>
<html>
<head>
  <title>
    It's going to rain
  </title>
</head>
<body>
  <article>
   <header>
     <h1>It's going to rain</h1>
```

```
<p>
<time pubdate datetime="2010-10-09T14:28-08:00"></time>
</p>
</header>
<p>Current forecast is for bigtime rain.</p>
<section>
 <h1>Comments</h1>
 <article>
  <footer>
   <p>Posted by: Sam Budd</p>
   <p><time pubdate datetime="2010-10-10T19:10-08:00">
   </time></p>
  </footer>
  <p>We need the rain.</p>
 </article>
 <article>
  <footer>
   <p>Posted by: Fred SMith</p>
   <p><time pubdate datetime="2010-10-10T19:15-08:00">
   </time></p>
  </footer>
  <p>Maybe you do. I don't.</p>
 </article>
 </section>
 </article>
 </body>
</htl>
```

The <aside> Element

The <aside> element represents an aside to the text, such as a sidebar. The text in an <aside> element is usually set off from the main body of text. Here are the attributes of this element:

- ▶ accesskey
- ▶ class
- ▶ contenteditable
- ▶ contextmenu
- ▶ dir
- ▶ draggable

- hidden
- id
- lang
- spellcheck
- style
- tabindex
- title

The <audio> Element

This element is covered in Lesson 8, "Using Video and Audio."

The <canvas> Element

This element is covered in Lesson 2, "Drawing with the Canvas Element."

The <command> Element

The <command> element can appear as a button, check box, or radio button. Here are the attributes:

- [accesskey
- [checked
- [class
- [contenteditable
- [contextmenu
- [dir
- [disabled
- [draggable

▶ [hidden

▶ [icon

▶ [id

▶ [label

▶ [lang

▶ radiogroup

▶ spellcheck

▶ style

▶ tabindex

▶ title

▶ type

The type attribute sets the type of control that will be displayed.

When the type attribute is set to "command" keyword, the control displays a button; the check box keyword maps to the Checkbox state, and the radio keyword maps to the Radio state.

Here's an example:

```
<menu type="toolbar">
  <command type="radio" radiogroup="colors" checked="checked"
    label="Left" onclick="red()">
  <command type="radio" radiogroup="colors"
    label="Center" onclick="blue()">
  <command type="radio" radiogroup="colors"
    label="Right" onclick="green()">
 <hr>
  <command type="command" disabled
    label="Publish" onclick="publish()">
</menu>
```

The <datalist> Element

The <datalist> element supplies <option> elements for other controls; you hook it up to <input> elements using the <input> elements' list attribute. Here are the attributes of this element:

- ▶ accesskey
- ▶ class
- ▶ contenteditable
- ▶ contextmenu
- ▶ dir
- ▶ draggable
- ▶ hidden
- ▶ id
- ▶ lang
- ▶ spellcheck
- ▶ style
- ▶ tabindex
- ▶ title

The <details> Element

The <details> element is a clickable element that opens to display more details when the user requests them. Here are the attributes of this element:

- ▶ accesskey
- ▶ class
- ▶ contenteditable
- ▶ contextmenu
- ▶ dir

- ► draggable

- ► hidden

- ► id

- ► lang

- ► open

- ► spellcheck

- ► style

- ► tabindex

- ► title

You store the actual details using <dt> (details title) and <dd> (details data elements). Here's an example:

```
<details>
  <summary>Ice Cream</summary>
  <dl>
    <dt>Flavor:</dt> <dd>Strawberry</dd>
    <dt>Name</dt> <dd>Big Red</dd>
    <dt>Contains Sugar</dt> <dd>Oh yes</dd>
  </dl>
</details>
</section>
```

The **<embed>** Element

The <embed> element lets you embed output from other applications, typically plug-ins, such as video or audio. Here are the attributes of this element:

- ► accesskey

- ► class

- ► contenteditable

- ► contextmenu

- ► dir

- ▶ draggable
- ▶ height
- ▶ hidden
- ▶ id
- ▶ lang
- ▶ spellcheck
- ▶ src
- ▶ style
- ▶ tabindex
- ▶ title
- ▶ type
- ▶ width

The src attribute gives the URL of the resource you want to embed. The type attribute should be set to the MIME type of the resource.

The <figcaption> Element

The <figcaption> element contains a figure caption for a <figure> element; see the <figure> element for more details. Here are the attributes of the <figcaption> element:

- ▶ accesskey
- ▶ class
- ▶ contenteditable
- ▶ contextmenu
- ▶ dir
- ▶ draggable
- ▶ hidden

- ▶ id
- ▶ lang
- ▶ spellcheck
- ▶ style
- ▶ tabindex
- ▶ title

The <figure> Element

The <figure> element lets you associate a figure caption with an image.
Here are the attributes of this element:

- ▶ accesskey
- ▶ class
- ▶ contenteditable
- ▶ contextmenu
- ▶ dir
- ▶ draggable
- ▶ hidden
- ▶ id
- ▶ lang
- ▶ spellcheck
- ▶ style
- ▶ tabindex
- ▶ title

Here's an example:

```
<figure>
```

```
<img src="icecream.jpeg"
    alt="Strawberry ice cream">
<figcaption>Strawberry ice cream</figcaption>
</figure>
```

The <footer> Element

This element lets you display text in a footer for the most recent <section>
element; here are the attributes of this element:

- ▶ accesskey
- ▶ class
- ▶ contenteditable
- ▶ contextmenu
- ▶ dir
- ▶ draggable
- ▶ hidden
- ▶ id
- ▶ lang
- ▶ spellcheck
- ▶ style
- ▶ tabindex
- ▶ title

See "The <article> Element" section for an example.

The <header> Element

This element groups together introductory and/or navigational material.
Here are the attributes of this element:

- ▶ accesskey

- ▶ class

- ▶ contenteditable

- ▶ contextmenu

- ▶ dir

- ▶ draggable

- ▶ hidden

- ▶ id

- ▶ lang

- ▶ spellcheck

- ▶ style

- ▶ tabindex

- ▶ title

Here's an example:

```
<body>
 <header>
  <h1>Ice Cream</h1>
  <nav>
   <ul>
    <li><a href="/strawberry">Strawberry</a>
    <li><a href="/chocolate">Chocolate</a>
    <li><a href="/vanilla">Vanilla</a>
   </ul>
  </nav>
  <h2>Good News About Ice Cream</h2>
 </header>
```

The <hgroup> Element

The <hgroup> element contains the heading of a section. The element is used to group a set of h1–h6 elements when the heading has multiple levels, such as subheadings, alternative titles, or taglines. Here are the attributes:

- ▶ accesskey
- ▶ class
- ▶ contenteditable
- ▶ contextmenu
- ▶ dir
- ▶ draggable
- ▶ hidden
- ▶ id
- ▶ lang
- ▶ spellcheck
- ▶ style
- ▶ tabindex
- ▶ title

You use this element to group multiple header elements as one as far as outlining programs are concerned.

The <keygen> Element

The <keygen> element represents a key/pair generator control for public and private keys. When the control's form is submitted, the private key is stored, and the public key is sent to the server. Here are the attributes of this element:

- ▶ accesskey
- ▶ autofocus

▶ challenge

▶ class

▶ contenteditable

▶ contextmenu

▶ dir

▶ disabled

▶ draggable

▶ form

▶ hidden

▶ id

▶ keytype

▶ lang

▶ name

▶ spellcheck

▶ style

▶ tabindex

▶ title

The <mark> Element

The <mark> element represents text in one document marked or highlighted for reference purposes because of its relevance in another context. Here are this element's attributes:

▶ accesskey

▶ class

▶ contenteditable

▶ contextmenu

- ▶ dir

- ▶ draggable

- ▶ hidden

- ▶ id

- ▶ lang

- ▶ spellcheck

- ▶ style

- ▶ tabindex

- ▶ title

Here's an example:

```
<p>The highlighted text below is the problem:</p>
<pre><code>
var x: Integer;
begin
   x := <mark>'a'</mark>;
end.
</code></pre>
```

The \<meter\> Element

The \<meter\> element displays a gauge that indicates how complete a measure or process is. The attributes of this element are the following:

- ▶ accesskey

- ▶ class

- ▶ contenteditable

- ▶ contextmenu

- ▶ dir

- ▶ draggable

- ▶ form

- hidden
- high
- id
- lang
- low
- max
- min
- optimum
- spellcheck
- style
- tabindex
- title
- value

Here's an example:

```
<meter min=0 max=60 value=15 title="Minutes"></meter>
```

The <nav> Element

The <nav> element contains navigation links; here are its attributes:

- accesskey
- class
- contenteditable
- contextmenu
- dir
- draggable
- hidden

- ▶ id

- ▶ lang

- ▶ spellcheck

- ▶ style

- ▶ tabindex

- ▶ title

And here's an example:

```
<body>
 <header>
  <nav>
  <h1>Ice Cream News</h1>
   <ul>
     <li><a href="articles.html">Index of all articles</a></li>
     <li><a href="today.html">Ice creeam issues today</a></li>
     <li><a href="new.html">New flavors</a></li>
   </ul>
  </nav>
 </header>
 <div>
        .
        .
        .
```

The <output> Element

The <output> element is a control that displays the result of a calculation. Here are its attributes:

- ▶ accesskey

- ▶ class

- ▶ contenteditable

- ▶ contextmenu

- ▶ dir

- ▶ draggable

- for

- form

- hidden

- id

- lang

- name

- spellcheck

- style

- tabindex

- title

Here's an example:

```
<form onsubmit="return false">
 <input name=x type=number step=any>
<br>
+
<br>
 <input name=y type=number step=any>
<br>
=
<br>
<output onforminput="value = x.value + y.value"></output>
</form>
```

It's not clear at this time how the <output> element will differ from a read-only text field.

The <progress> Element

The <progress> element displays a progress bar; here are this element's attributes:

- accesskey

- class

- ▶ contenteditable
- ▶ contextmenu
- ▶ dir
- ▶ draggable
- ▶ form
- ▶ hidden
- ▶ id
- ▶ lang
- ▶ max
- ▶ spellcheck
- ▶ style
- ▶ tabindex
- ▶ title
- ▶ value

Here's an example where you call a function named updateBar() to update the progress bar:

```
<head>
    <title>The Progress Bar</title>
    <script>
      var bar = document.getElementById('pb');
      function updateBar(new)
      {
         bar.value = new;
         bar.getElementsByTagName('span')[0].textContent =
            new;
      }
    </script>
</head>
<body>
    <h2>Task Progress</h2>
    <p>Progress: <progress id="pb"
    max=100><span>0</span>%</progress></p>
</body>
```

The **<rp>** Element

The <rp> element is part of the <ruby> element, which displays annotations for text (for example, ruby text is sometimes used to display pronunciation aids). The <rp> element encloses its text in parentheses inside the ruby text. Here are the attributes of this element:

- accesskey
- class
- contenteditable
- contextmenu
- dir
- draggable
- hidden
- id
- lang
- spellcheck
- style
- tabindex
- title

See the <ruby> element for more information.

The **<rt>** Element

The <rt> element marks the text component of a ruby annotation—see the <ruby> element for more information. Here are the attributes of the <rt> element:

- accesskey
- class
- contenteditable

▶ contextmenu

▶ dir

▶ draggable

▶ hidden

▶ id

▶ lang

▶ spellcheck

▶ style

▶ tabindex

▶ title

The <ruby> Element

Rubies display annotations, often pronunciation aids, next to the text they annotated. Here are the attributes of this element:

▶ accesskey

▶ class

▶ contenteditable

▶ contextmenu

▶ dir

▶ draggable

▶ hidden

▶ id

▶ lang

▶ spellcheck

▶ style

▶ tabindex

▶ title

The <section> Element

The <section> element represents a section of a body of text—for example, it could represent a chapter in a longer document. The <section> element is typically used to break up the <article> element into smaller divisions. Here are this element's attributes:

▶ accesskey

▶ class

▶ contenteditable

▶ contextmenu

▶ dir

▶ draggable

▶ hidden

▶ id

▶ lang

▶ spellcheck

▶ style

▶ tabindex

▶ title

See "The <article> Element" section for an example.

The **<source>** Element

The <source> element lets you specify multiple alternative media resources for media elements. In case one resource can't be found, the next one can be searched for. Here are the attributes of this element:

- ▶ accesskey
- ▶ class
- ▶ contenteditable
- ▶ contextmenu
- ▶ dir
- ▶ draggable
- ▶ hidden
- ▶ id
- ▶ lang
- ▶ media
- ▶ spellcheck
- ▶ src
- ▶ style
- ▶ tabindex
- ▶ title
- ▶ type

Here's an example:

```
<source src=icecream.mp4' type='video/mp4;
codecs="mp4v.20.240, mp4a.40.2"'>
```

The <summary> Element

The <summary> element is a child element of the <details> element and provides a summary of the content of the <details> element. Here are the <summary> element's attributes:

▶ accesskey

▶ class

▶ contenteditable

▶ contextmenu

▶ dir

▶ draggable

▶ hidden

▶ id

▶ lang

▶ spellcheck

▶ style

▶ tabindex

▶ title

The <time> Element

The <time> element contains a date stamp; here are its attributes:

▶ accesskey

▶ class

▶ contenteditable

▶ contextmenu

▶ datetime

▶ dir

▶ draggable

▶ hidden

▶ id

▶ lang

▶ pubdate

▶ spellcheck

▶ style

▶ tabindex

▶ title

And here is an example:

```
<time datetime="2010-10-09T14:28-08:00"></time>
```

The <video> Element

This element is covered in Lesson 8.

Index

FREE Online Edition

Your purchase of **Sams Teach Yourself HTML5 in 10 Minutes** includes access to a free online edition for 45 days through the Safari Books Online subscription service. Nearly every Sams book is available online through Safari Books Online, along with more than 5,000 other technical books and videos from publishers such as Addison-Wesley Professional, Cisco Press, Exam Cram, IBM Press, O'Reilly, Prentice Hall, and Que.

SAFARI BOOKS ONLINE allows you to search for a specific answer, cut and paste code, download chapters, and stay current with emerging technologies.

Activate your FREE Online Edition at www.informit.com/safarifree

> **STEP 1:** Enter the coupon code: HIOVXFA.

> **STEP 2:** New Safari users, complete the brief registration form. Safari subscribers, just log in.

If you have difficulty registering on Safari or accessing the online edition, please e-mail customer-service@safaribooksonline.com